VOLUME 7

NEW TESTAMENT

THE NEW COLLEGEVILLE BIBLE COMMENTARY

FIRST AND SECOND CORINTHIANS

Maria A. Pascuzzi

SERIES EDITOR

Daniel Durken, O.S.B.

LITURGICAL PRESS

Collegeville, Minnesota

www.litpress.org

Nihil obstat: Robert C. Harren, *Censor deputatus.*
Imprimatur: ✠ John F. Kinney, Bishop of St. Cloud, Minnesota, August 30, 2005.

Design by Ann Blattner.

Cover illustration: *Life in the Community* by Aidan Hart, in collaboration with Donald Jackson. Natural hand-ground ink on calfskin vellum, 15-7/8" X 24-1/2." Copyright 2005 *The Saint John's Bible* and the Hill Museum & Manuscript Library at Saint John's University, United States of America. Scripture quotations are from the New Revised Standard Version of the Bible, Catholic Edition, copyright © 1989, 1993 National Council of the Churches of Christ in the United States of America. Used by permission. All rights reserved.

Photos: pages 18, 47, 96, Jeffrey Hutson; pages 70, 126, David Manahan, o.s.b.; page 102, Corel Photos.

Scriptures selections are taken from the New American Bible Copyright © 1991, 1986, 1970 by the Confraternity of Christian Doctrine, 3211 Fourth Street, NE, Washington, DC 20017-1194 and are used by license of copyright owner. All rights reserved. No part of the New American Bible may be reproduced in any form or by any means without permission in writing from the copyright owner.

1	2	3	4	5	6	7	8	9

Library of Congress Cataloging-in-Publication Data

Pascuzzi, Maria.
    First and Second Corinthians / Maria A. Pascuzzi.
        p.   cm. — (The new Collegeville Bible commentary. New Testament ; v. 7)
        Summary: "Complete biblical texts with sound, scholarly based commentary that is written at a pastoral level; the Scripture translation is that of the New American Bible with Revised New Testament and Revised Psalms (1991)"—Provided by publisher.
        Includes bibliographical references.
        ISBN-13: 978-0-8146-2866-9 (pbk. : alk. paper)
        ISBN-10: 0-8146-2866-4 (pbk. : alk. paper)
    1. Bible. N.T. Corinthians, 1st—Commentaries.   2. Bible. N.T. Corinthians, 2nd—Commentaries.   I. Title.   II. Series.

BS2675.53.P37 2005
227'.2077—dc22

              2005007466

CONTENTS

ABBREVIATIONS

Books of the Bible

Acts—Acts of the Apostles
Amos—Amos
Bar—Baruch
1 Chr—1 Chronicles
2 Chr—2 Chronicles
Col—Colossians
1 Cor—1 Corinthians
2 Cor—2 Corinthians
Dan—Daniel
Deut—Deuteronomy
Eccl (or Qoh)—Ecclesiastes
Eph—Ephesians
Esth—Esther
Exod—Exodus
Ezek—Ezekiel
Ezra—Ezra
Gal—Galatians
Gen—Genesis
Hab—Habakkuk
Hag—Haggai
Heb—Hebrews
Hos—Hosea
Isa—Isaiah
Jas—James
Jdt—Judith
Jer—Jeremiah
Job—Job
Joel—Joel
John—John
1 John—1 John
2 John—2 John
3 John—3 John
Jonah—Jonah
Josh—Joshua
Jude—Jude
Judg—Judges
1 Kgs—1 Kings

2 Kgs—2 Kings
Lam—Lamentations
Lev—Leviticus
Luke—Luke
1 Macc—1 Maccabees
2 Macc—2 Maccabees
Mal—Malachi
Mark—Mark
Matt—Matthew
Mic—Micah
Nah—Nahum
Neh—Nehemiah
Num—Numbers
Obad—Obadiah
1 Pet—1 Peter
2 Pet—2 Peter
Phil—Philippians
Phlm—Philemon
Prov—Proverbs
Ps(s)—Psalms
Rev—Revelation
Rom—Romans
Ruth—Ruth
1 Sam—1 Samuel
2 Sam—2 Samuel
Sir—Sirach
Song—Song of Songs
1 Thess—1 Thessalonians
2 Thess—2 Thessalonians
1 Tim—1 Timothy
2 Tim—2 Timothy
Titus—Titus
Tob—Tobit
Wis—Wisdom
Zech—Zechariah
Zeph—Zephaniah

The Letters to the Corinthians

First and Second Corinthians are literary windows affording readers a "Paul's-eye" view into the life and development of one very dynamic Christian community. As we peer through them, what we see can quickly challenge idealized notions about the cohesiveness and harmony of the earliest communities of believers (cf. Acts 4:32). The way Paul tells it, the community at Corinth was characterized by rivalry (1 Cor 1:12); obsession with status and superior wisdom leading to arrogance (1 Cor 1–4); disregard for the less spiritually enlightened and gifted (1 Cor 8:1-13; 12–14) as well as for the economic have-nots (1 Cor 11:17-22); sexual immorality (1 Cor 5:1-13; 6:12-20); assertiveness with regard to individual rights (1 Cor 6:12-13); and, as time went on, a suspicious and disdainful attitude toward Paul himself (2 Cor 1:12–2:12; 10–12).

Such behavior serves to remind the reader that conversion did not produce an immediate social and moral transformation to a new way of life rooted in gospel values. Paul had to deal with this reality, and in his correspondence he commands, exhorts, persuades, threatens, does everything possible to refocus the community on the gospel and bring about transformed gospel living.

While these letters serve as windows on the past, they also reflect back to us much that still characterizes Christian living today. As we attempt now to understand the conflicting impulses, values, and behavior that gave rise to what Paul perceived as inauthentic Christian living at Corinth, perhaps we can better understand what contributes to inauthentic Christian living in our own day. We may also find in Paul's exigent call to the Corinthians to transform their lives the impetus for our own continued transformation in light of the gospel. Before examining each letter, some preliminary information about Corinth, Paul's work there, and the nature and purpose of the letters is needed to establish a context in which these letters can be more adequately understood.

The city of Corinth and its citizens

Corinth was strategically located on a narrow isthmus that linked mainland Greece to its north with the Peloponnesus to its south. The city was also an important east-west axis, located within a few miles of two great harbors: Cenchreae, which handled commerce to and from points east, and Lechaeum, which handled commerce to and from points west. This Greek city flourished from the fifth century B.C. until it was left in near ruin by the Romans in 146 B.C. A century passed before Corinth was refounded as a Roman colony in 44 B.C. The city was rebuilt according to Roman architectural patterns, reorganized politically in line with Roman government structures, and repopulated with Rome's urban poor, freedmen (former slaves), and slaves from among its conquered populations, as well as immigrants from the east, including Jews. Greek descendants of those who had survived Corinth's assault continued to live amidst its ruins. However, in this new Roman Corinth, they were regarded as resident aliens.

Within a few decades of its refounding, Corinth became the capital of the new Roman province Achaia. By the time Paul arrived, about A.D. 50/51, Corinth was emerging as Greece's premier city and the commercial, manufacturing, and cultural megacenter of the entire eastern Mediterranean. The stamp of Imperial Rome, as well as the influx of tradespersons, merchants, and tourists who came to visit Corinth's numerous shrines or to attend the Isthmian games, philosophers, and orators were all factors that contributed to the variety of ideas, mores, and perspectives that gave Corinth its vitality and appeal.

Paul's move to Corinth was probably calculated. The city's pluralistic and cosmopolitan character was clearly advantageous to him. He would no doubt get a hearing, and even a modestly successful mission among such sophisticated city-dwellers could lend credibility to his gospel of a crucified Messiah and validate his Gentile mission.

However, pluralism and sophistication were only two aspects of the social and the cultural ethos that dominated Corinth. The Corinthians were known to be fiercely competitive, driven by the desire for status, wealth, honor, and power. The route to these involved navigating the Roman patronage system, a network of hierarchically ordered patron-client relations. In return for the benefactions and enhanced social status gained through access to a rich patron's circle of influence, clients supported and promoted the patron, bolstering his status and ultimately widening his sphere of power.

Judging from Paul's description of the situation in the community, as noted above, it appears that these ingrained primary social and cultural values were carried over into the Christian community by the newly converted, with negative consequences. Their behavior, still conditioned by Corinth's secular values and aspirations, was destroying God's *ekklēsia*, a microsociety whose unity and holiness were to distinguish it from the macrosociety from which the converts came.

In these letters Paul negotiates the problems arising from this clash of values and deals with their negative impact on the life of the community. However, his greater concern is to further the process of resocialization by inculcating a perspective rooted in the gospel and the values and behavior consonant with that. This was no easy task, since Paul needed to remove Corinth's ethos from the Corinthians without removing the Corinthians from pagan Corinth (see 1 Cor 5:9-10)!

Paul's mission in Corinth and the Corinthian church

The Acts of the Apostles, a key secondary source for Paul's life and work after his own letters, provides scant information about Paul's founding mission in Corinth. He came to Corinth after a short and largely unsuccessful stay in Athens (Acts 17:15-34). He found lodging and work as a tentmaker with Priscilla and Aquila, a Jewish-Christian couple, and was soon joined by his co-workers Silas and Timothy (Acts 18:1-5). According to Luke, Paul began evangelizing in the synagogue, but as Jewish opposition increased, he refocused his efforts on the Gentiles and moved his ministry base to the home of a Gentile believer, Titus Justus (Acts 18:5-8). Luke reports that Paul ministered at Corinth for a year and a half (Acts 18:11), but without specifying dates for this sojourn. The mention of Paul's arraignment before Gallio (Acts 18:12-17), proconsul of Achaia from either A.D. 50 to 51 or 51 to 52, has figured significantly in attempts to date Paul's ministry in Corinth, which many scholars place sometime between A.D. 50 and 52.

More insight about Paul's life and ministry at Corinth and the composition of the community is gained from the Corinthian correspondence itself. Paul declares that he had come to preach, not baptize, though he admits baptizing a few, perhaps in the earliest days of his ministry (1 Cor 1:14-17). By deliberate choice, he preached his gospel without eloquence (1 Cor 1:17; 2:1-5). Just how rhetorically unimpressive Paul was is hard to say. However, he may have been outclassed in the eyes of the community by a certain Apollos, famed for eloquence, who preached at Corinth after Paul's departure (Acts 18:24; 19:1; 1 Cor 3:6). Paul testifies that he worked to support himself so that he could preach his gospel to all free of charge (1 Corinthians 9). This may reflect his deliberate choice to avoid entanglement in the patronage system with its obligation. Both Paul's choice to forego financial support as well as his alleged lack of rhetorical prowess are issues that will surface again in 2 Corinthians 10–12.

With regard to the community, composed of Jews and Gentiles, the latter apparently predominated, judging by the decidedly pagan aspect of the issues Paul treated, for example, food sacrificed to idols and attendance at pagan temple feasts (1 Cor 8–10), as well as references to their former idolatrous way of life (1 Cor 6:10; 8:7; 12:2). Past assumptions that community members were drawn from Corinth's lower classes, largely based on remarks about their insignificant origins and status (1 Cor 1:26-31), have been modified in view of recent research into the social composition of urban Christian communities. It is now acknowledged that along with the economically poor, the Corinthian community included others disadvantaged because of ethnicity, class, or gender biases, and still others considered to be persons of some means and social stature who are mentioned in the text (e.g., 1 Cor 1:14; 16:17, 19; see further Rom 16:1, 21-23).

Given the diversity of this community, estimated to number anywhere from fifty to two hundred persons, scholars prefer to speak of it as "socially stratified." This socioeconomic diversity probably accounts for community tensions at the Lord's Supper, where the poor were disregarded (1 Cor 11:17-22), and other situations where some members may have used their means or status to the detriment of others (e.g., 1 Cor 6:1-11) or to exempt themselves from certain moral dictates (e.g., 1 Cor 5:1-13).

The nature and purpose of Paul's Letters to the Corinthians

Paul wrote 1 Corinthians from Ephesus about A.D. 55/56. Second Corinthians was written a year or so later from Macedonia after Paul received Titus's update on the situation at Corinth. Evidence in these letters indicates that Paul had actually written more than two letters to this community. In 1 Corinthians 5:9, Paul states that he had written a previous letter, no longer extant, containing information relevant to an issue he was now writing about in 1 Corinthians 5. Then, in 2 Corinthians 2:1-4, he speaks of a "tearful letter," obviously predating 2 Corinthians. Attempts have been made to identify this "tearful letter" with 1 Corinthians or with 2 Corinthians 10–13. However, both identifications have been seriously questioned, and the possibility that the "tearful letter" is also lost cannot be excluded.

Many scholars have argued that 2 Corinthians is a combination of at least two letters: 2 Corinthians 1–9 plus 2 Corinthians 10–13. Others have suggested five or six. What is important to recognize here is that 1 and 2 Corinthians are only part of a continuous dialogue between Paul and this community. Fortunately, they are preserved in the canon of the New Testament, where they are designated "first" and "second" in view of their respective lengths. However, they were not necessarily letters one and two in Paul's ongoing correspondence with the community, which included at least four letters.

First and Second Corinthians are true letters reflecting contemporary Greco-Roman conventions of letter writing. Each letter has an opening section with its requisite features, a body, the main part of the letter, where key matters are taken up, and a conclusion. These and other formal and stylistic features will be noted in the course of the commentary. Here it is important to underscore that in Paul's day the letter functioned as a substitute for personal presence when this was not possible (1 Cor 5:3) or, in some cases, not desirable (2 Cor 2:1-2). In 1 and 2 Corinthians, we read what Paul wanted to say about issues and developments in the community articulated from his point of view. In other words, we read only one-half of a dialogue between partners involved in an ongoing relationship. Many details and facts already known to Paul and the Corinthians are omitted. At times Paul quotes the Corinthians (e.g., 1 Cor 6:12; 7:1) and offers clues about the evolving situation there (e.g., 2 Cor 11:4-15). These do illumine some Corinthian views and some of the content and contours of Paul's own remarks. However, a fuller picture of the situation depends, to a large extent, on the piecing together of textual and extratextual clues.

It is a commonplace in Pauline studies to refer to Paul's writings as "occasional letters." What is recognized in the use of this term is that his letters were prompted, or occasioned, by particular circumstances, questions, or behavior arising in the daily life of the communities Paul had founded that necessitated a response from him. They are not sustained and systematic expositions of Paul's accumulated theological insights. Even Romans, the one letter written by Paul to a community he had not founded, is now considered to have more of an occasional character than previously assumed.

Thus, what we find in 1 and 2 Corinthians are *ad hoc* responses intended primarily for a particular community and its peculiar needs. This is not to suggest that Paul lacked any theological framework within which he formulated his responses. Rather, it is to caution against assuming that what we read is Paul's coherently articulated and exhaustive last word on all issues. It is more likely we are reading Paul's first word on a variety of issues, most of which arose only after he had moved on to evangelize elsewhere.

Though a letter and a speech were not identical, the letter substituted for speech, as noted above. In Paul's day, speech was of utmost importance. Political leaders, as well as those who claimed to teach religious and philosophical truths, were expected to speak eloquently and persuasively.

Rhetoric, the study of how to argue persuasively in a given situation, was a main component of Greco-Roman education. Though it was primarily concerned with techniques for researching, constructing, and ultimately delivering a winning speech, its aims and conventions also affected how people wrote. Given this overlap between speech and letter and the fact that Paul designed his letters to be read aloud (Phlm 2; 1 Thess 5:27), it is reasonable to expect that Paul employed contemporary techniques of argumentation to make as persuasive a case as possible for his own points.

Speeches, or arguments, were classified according to three types, each ordered to a distinct purpose and appropriate to a different setting. The forensic or judicial speech, proper to the courtroom, was used to defend or accuse someone in view of a past action. The deliberative speech, for use in the assembly, sought to persuade or dissuade about future courses of action. Finally, epideictic speech, appropriate for a variety of public occasions, employed praise or blame to affirm important values and reinforce the audience's current adherence to them. Speeches normally began with an introduction and concluded with a recapitulation of key points. In between, other standardized components were incorporated depending on the type of argument. However, every argument had two indispensable parts: a statement of the thesis/point to be proved, followed by the proofs. Persuasion, regardless of the speech type, ultimately depended on three factors: the moral character of the speaker, or proof based on *ethos;* the ability to evoke the proper emotional response from the audience, or proof based on *pathos;* and finally logical arguments, or proof based on *logos.*

With regard to the Corinthian correspondence, the deliberative type of argument is dominant in 1 Corinthians, where Paul frequently attempts to persuade or dissuade the community about possible courses of action in view of what is advantageous to the community (e.g., 1 Cor 7; 8–10; 12–14). At certain points, he also introduces forensic and epideictic rhetoric as the situation demands (e.g., 1 Cor 5; 9; 13).

In 2 Corinthians we come across a changed situation. A wedge has been driven between Paul and the community by outsiders. Speaking in his own defense, Paul employs forensic rhetoric at 2 Corinthians 1:1–7:6 and again at 2 Corinthians 10–13. In 2 Corinthians 8–9, Paul deliberates with the community, urging it to go forward with a planned collection that will benefit both the impoverished community at Jerusalem and the Corinthians themselves, who will be distinguished for their generosity.

Throughout these two letters Paul's appeals to his own character and to the emotions of the community are deftly interwoven with logical arguments, evidencing both Paul's rhetorical sophistication and his intention to persuade rather than simply impose his will. Recognition of the rhetorical nature of 1 and 2 Corinthians contributes to a more informed and profitable reading of these letters, which are composed of discreet argumentative units where Paul is engaged in persuasion.

The occasion and structure of I Corinthians

Sometime after Paul had left Corinth and was settled into his ministry at Ephesus, oral and written reports about a number of developments in the community at Corinth reached him. Through "Chloe's people," that is, members of her household, Paul was orally apprised of rivalries within the community (1 Cor 1:11). He says that he had also heard about a case of sexual immorality (1 Cor 5:2) and divisions at the Eucharist (1 Cor 11:18). Chloe's people or others could have been the source of this information. Other information, whose source is unspecified, concerning lawsuits (6:1-11), fornication (6:12-20), inappropriate attire at the liturgy (11:2-16), and disagreement over the resurrection (1 Cor 15) may have also been referred to Paul orally.

Paul's second source of information was a letter written by the Corinthians asking his advice on various issues (1 Cor 7:1). Their questions related to matters ranging from sex within marriage, which, apparently, some wanted to renounce (1 Cor 7:2-6), to the advisability of marriage (7:7-40), to whether one could eat food offered to idols (1 Cor 8), to the use of spiritual gifts (1 Cor 12–14). This letter was brought to Paul by community delegates, presumably the persons Paul mentions at 1 Corinthians 16:17. In addition to Chloe's people, this delegation may also have supplied some of the oral information. As a response to the information that had reached him, Paul composed 1 Corinthians.

To explain the ideological basis that influenced the thought and motivated the behavior reflected in 1 Corinthians, some scholars have hypothesized that some group (e.g., Gnostics or Judaizers) or person (e.g., Apollos) from outside the community introduced ideas at variance with what Paul had preached. Others explain the problems as deriving from "overrealized eschatology," that is, the Corinthians misinterpreted Paul's message, incorrectly assuming that they were already fully transformed and free of all moral constraints. Another explanation holds that the Corinthians understood Paul, lived according to what he had preached, but that Paul, for political reasons, changed his mind about things and now saw their behavior as a problem.

Each theory has been subjected to scrutiny and found to be inadequate. What seems apparent from 1 Corinthians is that here we encounter real flesh-and-blood people working out the implications of their new faith. In light of more recent investigations into the social and cultural ethos of the Corinthians, it is possible to understand the Corinthian situation as testimony to the difficulties that accompanied the planting of the Christian gospel in a pagan environment such as Corinth, where environmental influences were still strong. The difficulties Paul addresses in this letter are not between the community and himself, but rather within this nascent community struggling with its own identity, ethos, and behavior.

In 1 Corinthians, Paul deals with a larger number of disparate issues than in any other of his letters. The variety of issues, along with what scholars perceived as multiple literary and logical incongruities (e.g., contradictory responses on idol meat at chs. 8 and 10), led to speculation that 1 Corinthians was a compilation of letters. This hypothesis has proved to be unwarranted, especially in view of more recent insights about how Paul unfolds his arguments. Most scholars now affirm the literary unity of first Corinthians.

Nonetheless, it is still not easy to fathom the letter's logic as Paul shifts from topic to topic. A variety of ways of understanding the letter's structural organization have been proposed. Many understand 1 Corinthians to consist of an introduction (1:1-9) and conclusion (16:1-21) enclosing the body of the letter, which is envisioned according to a two-part structure: responses to matters referred orally to Paul (1:10-6:20), followed by responses to the Corinthians' letter (7:1–15:58). The phrase "now in regard . . . " (e.g., 7:1, 25; 12:1) is usually taken to signal the beginning of Paul's response to a question or issue raised in the letter.

Currently, there is a growing tendency to understand the structure of 1 Corinthians along the lines of a deliberative speech. Paul's exhortation "that there be no divisions . . . that you be united in the same mind and in the same purpose" (1:10) is construed as his major thesis. The body of the letter consists of a series of rhetorical proofs or demonstrations in support of the thesis (1:11–15:58). The thesis plus demonstrations are encompassed by the exordium at 1:1-9 (the rhetorical equivalent of the literary introduction) and the recapitulation at 16:13-18 (the argument's conclusion). Understood from the vantage point of rhetoric, 1 Corinthians is a sustained argument on the single theme of unity, cast in the form of a deliberative speech.

The two-part literary schema and the rhetorical schema are both useful for understanding the letter's structure, provided we recognize that neither accounts perfectly for its structure and we do not adhere too rigidly to either one. In the case of the two-part schema, an "oral matter" intrudes on the written responses at 11:18. Additionally, there is no indication that the discussion on hairstyles at 11:2-16 or on the resurrection at chapter 15 is actually a response to a written inquiry. In the case of the rhetorical schema, while chapters 1–4 clearly relate to the problem of factionalism and support Paul's call for unity, not every piece of advice or resolution of a problem found throughout 1 Corinthians 5–16 is constructed in view of resolving the problem of factionalism (e.g., ch. 7). In fact, in 1 Corinthians 5–16, Paul is not always deliberating (e.g., chs. 5, 9, and 13). Thus, rather than insisting on either structural schema, it may be more useful to focus on the discrete units or blocks of argumentation contained in 1 Corinthians. Careful examination of their content, as well as Paul's persuasive strategy, should allow us to apprehend Paul's major concerns in this letter.

A final point of consideration regarding the structure of 1 Corinthians concerns a compositional pattern Paul uses to arrange his thought, which is especially recurrent in this letter. The pattern is evidenced when Paul introduces a topic, (A), shifts to another topic, (B), then returns to his original topic, (A'); hence the designation ABA', or concentric pattern. 1 Corinthians 8–10 is a good example. Paul discusses idol meat in chapter 8, (A), shifts to discuss his apostolic rights in chapter 9, (B), then returns to idol meat in chapter 10, (A'). As scholars now recognize, the B section, once perceived to rupture the flow of Paul's thought, actually reinforces the point being made in the adjacent A and A' sections. The B section is an example of the rhetorical technique "digression," an insertion into an argument to amplify or support the main point. This way of unfolding an argument clearly contrasts with a linear arrangement of ideas to which modern readers are accustomed. However, it accorded with the accustomed literary and rhetorical methods of Paul's day. Once we understand Paul's method of unfolding an argument, both its coherence and its point become more readily apparent.

Paul's theological perspective in 1 Corinthians

Paul's responses to the Corinthians were shaped by the dialogue between himself and them, but they were rooted in Jewish tradition, enriched by Paul's understanding of what God had done in Christ. Paul shared with other Jews an apocalyptic view centered on the hope that God would intervene to overthrow the evil order now reigning in the world, after which a new order under God's sovereignty would be ushered in. According to Paul, God had powerfully intervened as hoped, but in an unexpected and paradoxical way through the mystery of Christ crucified (1:18). Christians were therefore living at a crucial juncture point: the world in its present form was passing away (7:31; 10:11), the new order was beginning (2 Cor 5:17b). For Paul, this entire transition hinged on Christ's death and resurrection, the eschatological (end-time) salvation event through which humanity gained the renewed existence that Jewish tradition associated with the end-time. The inauguration of the end-time would be signaled by the outpouring of the Spirit (1:7; 2:12; 3:16). Coincident with this salvation event, God was now calling into Christ's fellowship the new, end-time community (1:9).

Since Paul believed that all this had been accomplished through Christ, to whom the Corinthian community owed its existence, he brings his christological insights to bear on his responses to this community. Their human wisdom is revalued in light of God's wisdom and power shown forth in Christ crucified (1:18). Their boasting is shown to have no foundation, since everything comes from God in Christ (3:21-23; 4:7). Through Christ's death they have been washed, redeemed, sanctified (1:30; 5:7; 6:11) and brought back for God (6:19-20; 7:23). They are now the "church of God" (1:2), "God's temple" (3:17).

As a result, how the Corinthians behave can never be independent of God, under whose sovereignty they stand and by whose will they are called and empowered by the Spirit to live lives of holiness (1:2). In Christ, believers formed one body (12:12), a unity effected through baptism and manifested and reinforced by the Eucharist (10:16-17). Immorality that threatened the community's holiness had to be avoided (5:13; 6:18; 10:14). Likewise, unity-destroying distinctions and behavior, whether based on status (11:17-24), knowledge (ch. 8), or spiritual endowment (chs. 12 and 14), had to be abandoned. The well-being of the whole church would form the context for discernment and behavior (6:12b; 8:3; 10:24, 31-33; 14:12), motivated by love (ch. 13).

Paul stresses throughout 1 Corinthians that this eschatological existence is not yet complete (1:7-8). That would come in the future, when death would be conquered, physical bodies would be transformed into glorious resurrection bodies, and all things would be subjected to God through Christ (ch. 15). In the meantime, the Corinthians were to use the freedom wrought by Christ to preserve their holiness and unity, the twin hallmarks of God's eschatological community (see, e.g., Ezek 37:15-28). The extent to which Paul's commands and exhortations throughout 1 Corinthians are concerned with the true nature of the community underscores the centrality of ecclesiology in this letter. How should this community, poised between the event of Christ's death and resurrection and the promise of future glory, live in the present? Paul's concern in 1 Corinthians is to help the community with this perennially difficult question.

OUTLINE OF FIRST CORINTHIANS

1:1-9	*Introduction*
1:1-3	Greeting
1:4-9	Thanksgiving
1:10–4:21	*Argument for Unity in the Community*
1:10-17	Divisions in the community
1:18–2:5	The wisdom of the cross
2:6–3:4	The wisdom of the mature
3:5-23	The community and its leaders
4:1-21	Cross-wisdom: the ultimate critique
5:1–6:20	*Arguments Concerning Immorality within the Community and Relationships with Those Outside the Community*
5:1-13	Argument against sexual immorality
6:1-11	Argument against recourse to pagan courts
6:12-20	Argument against sexual immorality
7:1-40	*Concerning Marriage and Sexual Relations*
7:1-16	Advice to the married, unmarried, and widows
7:17-24	Advice on one's social status
7:25-40	Advice to virgins/engaged couples, married women, and widows
8:1–11:1	*Argument Concerning Food Offered to Idols*
8:1-13	Concern for others trumps knowledge as a criterion for action
9:1-27	Renunciation of rights: an illustration based on Paul's praxis
10:1-13	Complacency and God's wrath: an example based on Israel's past
10:14-22	Against communion with idols: judge for yourselves
10:23–11:1	Summary: seek the good of others
11:2–14:40	*Arguments Concerning Aspects of Community Worship*
11:2-16	Argument concerning hairstyles
11:17-34	Argument concerning division and abuses at the Lord's Supper
12:1–14:40	Argument concerning spiritual gifts
15:1-58	*Argument for the Resurrection*
15:1-11	The resurrection of Christ: rehearsing the facts
15:12-34	The reality of the resurrection of the dead

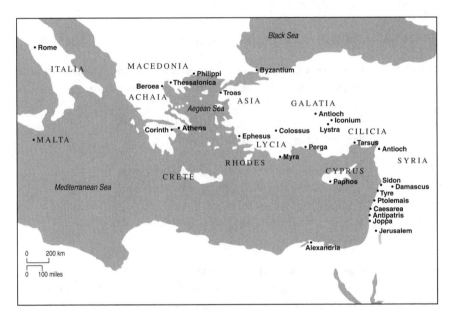

The World of Paul

The First Letter to the Corinthians

I. Address

1 **Greeting.** ¹Paul, called to be an apostle of Christ Jesus by the will of God, and Sosthenes our brother, ²to the church of God that is in Corinth, to you who have been sanctified in Christ Jesus, called to be holy, with all those everywhere who call upon the name of our Lord Jesus Christ, their Lord and ours. ³Grace to you and peace from God our Father and the Lord Jesus Christ.

INTRODUCTION

1 Corinthians 1:1-9

1:1-3 Greeting

The opening section of an ancient letter consisted of three parts: the name of the sender, the name of the recipients, and a greeting. Paul follows this convention, naming himself and Sosthenes as the letter's co-senders. Co-sender need not imply that Sosthenes was co-author of this letter. Throughout 1 Corinthians, the first person "I" dominates. This suggests that a single author, Paul, was responsible for the composition and content of the letter. Moreover, even when the plural is used, what is usually intended is the whole community of Christians, for example, "are we provoking the Lord?" (10:22).

Paul adds a description of himself that is brief but dense with insight into his self-understanding. He is first of all an "apostle," a term that is both a title and a description of a function. It derives from the Greek verb *apostellō*, which means "to send." Used in conjunction with the phrase "of Jesus Christ," here the term "apostle" denotes Paul's function as one sent out on behalf of, or as an envoy of, Jesus Christ. Paul does not appropriate

▶ This symbol indicates a cross reference number in the *Catechism of the Catholic Church*. See page 151 for number citations.

Thanksgiving. ⁴I give thanks to my God always on your account for the grace of God bestowed on you in Christ Jesus, ⁵that in him you were enriched in every way, with all discourse and all knowledge, ⁶as the testimony to Christ

---

this function for himself; rather, it is enjoined on him as one "called" to be Christ's envoy "by the will of God" (see further Gal 1:15). By underscoring the divine initiative, Paul reminds the Corinthians that he is an authorized envoy of Christ, in whose name and by whose authority he worked among them and now writes to them. Stated from the perspective of rhetoric, Paul has established his *ethos* here. This will serve as an important argument throughout the letter.

Unless the Sosthenes mentioned in 1:1 is the same Sosthenes named in the Acts of the Apostles, we have no information concerning his identity. In Acts 18:17, Sosthenes, a synagogue official at Corinth, is mentioned in the context of Paul's arraignment before Gallio, the proconsul. After Gallio had refused to hear the case against Paul brought by the Jews and had ejected them from the tribunal (Acts 18:15-16), the Jews seized Sosthenes and beat him. Whether Sosthenes was beaten because he was sympathetic to Paul is not known. Nor is it ever recounted in Acts or elsewhere that this particular Sosthenes converted to Christianity. Thus there are no compelling reasons to identify the Sosthenes of Acts 18:17 with the person mentioned at 1:1 who is also called by this commonly used name. The most we can deduce from 1:1 is that this Sosthenes was in Ephesus with Paul. Given the fact that Paul adds no other information about him, either here or in the rest of 1 Corinthians, it is also reasonable to deduce that the Corinthian community was familiar with this Sosthenes, called "our brother," a term used for fellow believers and co-workers.

Paul identifies the recipients of this letter as the "church of God that is in Corinth" (1:2). The term *ekklēsia,* which can be translated "church," "assembly," or "congregation," was used in secular Greek to refer to a political assembly. Paul distinguishes his addressees as the *ekklēsia* "of God," which exists not by self-determination or in view of common political concerns, but because God has called it into being.

This theological qualification of the community is augmented by three others. First, the community is sanctified, that is, made holy or set apart for God in Christ Jesus, through whom they have received this new identity. Second, they are called to be holy. This is not a mere rephrasing of the previous qualification; rather, it defines how the community must live in view of the fact that it has been sanctified. Finally, the community at Corinth

19

The wide Lechaion Road in Corinth linked the port to the marketplace, or agora.

was confirmed among you, [7] so that you are not lacking in any spiritual gift as you wait for the revelation of our Lord Jesus Christ. [8] He will keep you firm to the end, irreproachable on the day of our Lord Jesus [Christ]. [9] God is faithful, and by him you were called to fellowship with his Son, Jesus Christ our Lord.

---

does not exist independently but is part of a universal fellowship of believers who call upon the name of the Lord and are subject to his authority. These theological, christological, and ecclesiological qualifications ascribed to the community at the outset of the letter influence all that follows.

Paul concludes this opening section with his characteristic grace and peace greeting. Rather than the usual Greek *chair* ("to rejoice"), Paul substitutes *charis* ("grace") and adds the Jewish greeting *shalom* ("peace"). *Charis* expresses Paul's understanding of how God acts toward humanity, in infinite generosity. *Shalom* expresses the result of God's generous activity, humanity's entire well-being that comes from God through Christ.

1:4-9 Thanksgiving

Paul's thanksgiving section adheres to the ancient letter form in which some type of thanksgiving followed the opening formula. Paul's thanks are directed to God, the source and bestower of the grace the Corinthians have received. This grace has taken the form of enrichment in every spiritual gift, especially in "discourse" (speech) and "knowledge." Paul, who is himself spiritually enriched (14:18), is genuinely grateful to God that the Corinthians enjoy such blessing. Indeed, these gifts confirm Paul's testimony to Christ and verify that the gospel has taken root among the Corinthians (1:6). Yet Paul knows that the full outworking of God's purposes lies beyond the present and the Corinthians' current state of spiritual endowment. The Corinthians must still await the final revelation of Jesus Christ and continually rely on the work of Christ to keep them irreproachable until that day of judgment (1:7-8). Paul's thanksgiving ends on a note of confidence, because "God is faithful" and called the Corinthians into fellowship *(koinōnia)* with Jesus Christ.

Within this section Paul introduces some key theological points that anticipate issues to be addressed in this letter. His thanksgiving to God for the bestowal of grace contrasts with the Corinthians' boastful attitude, for which Paul will repeatedly chide the community, reminding them that everything they have is a gift from God through Christ (4:7). The very gifts for which Paul expresses thanks will unfortunately turn out to be a source of division in the community. Paul will have to address this and remind the Corinthians that every gift comes from the same Spirit (12:4), is set at

II. Disorders in the Corinthian Community

A. Divisions in the Church

Groups and Slogans. [10]I urge you, brothers, in the name of our Lord Jesus Christ, that all of you agree in what you say, and that there be no divisions among you, but that you be united in the same mind and in the same purpose. [11]For it has been reported to me about you, my brothers, by Chloe's people, that there are rivalries among you. [12]I mean that each of you is saying, "I belong to Paul," or "I belong to Apollos," or "I belong to Cephas," or "I be-

---

the service of the same Lord (12:5), and is ordered to the welfare of the whole body of believers (12:12-26).

Likewise, the eschatological perspective that circumscribes the thanksgiving will be brought forward in Paul's attempts to redress the problems that derive from the Corinthians' over satisfaction with their current spiritual status. Paul will repeatedly remind the community that the future eschatological event impinges on how they live and behave in the present (4:5; 6:13-14; 7:29-35). Finally, of overriding importance in the rest of 1 Corinthians is the fact that the Corinthians are divinely created in fellowship with Christ. This fellowship with, or participation in, the life of the risen Jesus is the basis for their hope of future glory (15:20). However, participation also enjoins upon each believer the ongoing task of realizing this fellowship. In some way or another, the reality of this fellowship will pervade Paul's responses throughout the letter.

ARGUMENT FOR UNITY IN THE COMMUNITY

1 Corinthians 1:10–4:21

This first major section of the letter body forms a coherent unit revolving around Paul's call for unity in the face of reported divisions within the community. Apparently, multiple factors are behind the divisiveness: attachment to particular teachers, pursuit of wisdom apart from the wisdom of the crucified Christ that Paul has preached, and boasting in status. In his effort to move the Corinthians to restore unity, Paul will have to clear up two misconceptions—one relating to the nature of the gospel, the other to the role of ministers.

Divisions in the community (1:10-17)

1:10-17 Report of rivalries

Paul begins with an urgent plea in the name of the Lord Jesus, under whose authority the Corinthians stand, that they let go of their divisions

long to Christ." [13]Is Christ divided? Was Paul crucified for you? Or were you baptized in the name of Paul? [14]I give thanks [to God] that I baptized none of you except Crispus and Gaius, [15]so that no one can say you were baptized in my name. [16](I baptized the household of Stephanas also; beyond that I do not know whether I baptized anyone else.) [17]For Christ did not send me to baptize but to preach the gospel, and not with the wisdom of human eloquence, so that the cross of Christ might not be emptied of its meaning.

---

and be united. "United" translates a Greek verb that literally means "restore." Thus Paul is not urging the Corinthians to do something new but to restore the unity of mind and purpose proper to those called into fellowship with Christ. The source of Paul's information about the community situation is disclosed immediately—"Chloe's people." These associates of Chloe were likely traveling on her behalf from Ephesus to Corinth, where they observed the situation.

Returning to Ephesus, they reported to Paul, informing him of rivalries stemming from allegiances to particular persons. Some were identifying themselves with Paul, others with Apollos, others with Cephas, and some even claimed allegiance to Christ alone. The phrases "I belong to Paul . . . Cephas," etc., have been taken as the slogans of actual parties at Corinth, and great effort has been exerted to reconstruct the particular ideological bias of each group. However, Paul's use of these phrases may simply be his way of putting into his own words his understanding or interpretation of the situation. In fact, Paul's use of the introductory words "I mean that . . ." (v. 12) just before the mention of the so-called parties seems to indicate that we are hearing Paul's rearticulation of the report about rivalries which he construes in relation to four figures.

Clearly there were divisions in the community that may have revolved around the favoring of some person over another (vv. 11-13), which may have been linked to who baptized whom (vv. 13-16). Additionally, Paul's contrast between the cross of Christ and the wisdom of human eloquence (v. 17) suggests that this, too, was at the root of the divisions. However, that the community was actually divided into four clearly delineated groups does not seem to have been the case. In fact, Paul never refers to them again in the letter. Paul's characterization of the situation in this way allows him to set the stage for his handling of the problem of disunity.

For Paul, it is simply inconceivable that Christians be divided at all, let alone on account of allegiance stemming from baptism, the sacrament that unites all believers to Christ and to one another. The series of rhetorical

◀ **Paradox of the Cross.** ¹⁸The message of the cross is foolishness to those who are perishing, but to us who are being saved it is the power of God. ¹⁹For it is written:

"I will destroy the wisdom of the wise,
and the learning of the learned
I will set aside."

²⁰Where is the wise one? Where is the scribe? Where is the debater of this age? Has not God made the wisdom of the world foolish? ²¹For since in the wisdom of God the world did not come to know God through wisdom, it was the will of God through the foolishness of the proclamation to save those who have faith. ²²For Jews demand signs

---

questions in 1:13 underscores the absurdity of partisanship. Christ is not divided, and neither can those baptized into Christ be divided! In an aside (vv. 14-16), Paul dissociates himself from baptism-based partisanship by disclaiming any extensive personal role in baptizing. This disclaimer introduces an opening for Paul to highlight what he is called and sent to do as an apostle: preach the gospel, and "not with the wisdom of human eloquence" (v. 17). With this negation, Paul rejects persuasive wisdom as antithetical to the wisdom of the cross that he preaches. This opposition seems to be at the root of divisions in the community that Paul deals with in the next step of his argument, where he will set out the essence of his gospel.

The wisdom of the cross (1:18–2:5)

In the foreground of this section of Paul's argument is the paradoxical message of the cross, God's wisdom and power (1:18-25). The Corinthians themselves are testimony to this message (1:26-31); its very essence accounts for Paul's preaching without persuasive words (2:1-5). Divisions, though not directly mentioned in this subsection, are in the background, since vain pursuit of human wisdom and boasting about those who make the best case for it are fundamental to the divisiveness.

1:18-25 The paradox of the cross

The gospel Paul preaches is Christ crucified, God's wisdom and power. God's cross-revealed wisdom defies human wisdom and divides humanity into two groups: the perishing, who reject this message as foolishness, and those being saved, for whom it is the power of God. The divine overthrow of human wisdom foretold by Isaiah (Isa 29:14) was taking place in the cross. Even the wise man, scholar, and philosopher, representatives of the sharpest thinkers of this age, are incapable of fathoming God's wisdom and power revealed in Christ crucified because theirs is human wisdom, originating in this age, which God has made

and Greeks look for wisdom, ²³but we proclaim Christ crucified, a stumbling block to Jews and foolishness to Gentiles, ²⁴but to those who are called, Jews and Greeks alike, Christ the power of God and the wisdom of God. ²⁵For the foolishness of God is wiser than human wisdom, and the weakness of God is stronger than human strength.

The Corinthians and Paul. ²⁶Consider your own calling, brothers. Not many of you were wise by human

---

foolish (1:21). According to human categories, crucifixion, epitomizing weakness and suffering, simply cannot cash out as any kind of wisdom or power, let alone divine wisdom and power!

Humankind's objections to this message are ethnically and historically particularized in the reactions of Jews and Greeks. Jews want signs. Accustomed to a God who had worked wonderfully and powerfully to deliver and save Israel in the past, Jews simply cannot see in a crucified Messiah the power and wisdom of God. For them, the cross is an affront, a stumbling block (see Rom 9:32-33; 11:11). Greeks, on the other hand, want wisdom, that is, the insights and strategies that lead to power, success, and honor. In Greco-Roman society in general, and in Corinth in particular, these were considered the manifestations of the truly wise person. For such as these, the cross signified everything that was counter to wisdom; cross-wisdom was an oxymoron, sheer foolishness. Despite the fact that Jews and Greeks differed with regard to how divine wisdom and power should be authenticated, they were in agreement that it would have to be authenticated by something other than the mind-boggling paradox of the cross.

Yet, it is precisely through what both reject that both Jews and Greeks are saved. Therefore, despite their expectations, Paul insists, "we" preach Christ crucified, a message that disregards humanly established ways of knowing God's power and wisdom, which are known in the cross or not at all. Humans must either give up their categories and accept the crucified Christ as the means of salvation or keep to their own standards, rejecting the message of the cross and perishing. In summarizing his reflections, Paul restates the paradox of the cross. Its very weakness is God's power, more powerful than human strength. Its very absurdity is God's wisdom, wiser than human wisdom. This is the gospel. It runs counter to the world's wisdom. It is fathomed by those willing to see differently and able to live in the tension of this paradox.

1:26-31 The experience of the Corinthians

This paradox is now considered in light of the Corinthians' own experience. Before their call, many were the world's nobodies. So little is

standards, not many were powerful, not many were of noble birth. ²⁷Rather, God chose the foolish of the world to shame the wise, and God chose the weak of the world to shame the strong, ²⁸and God chose the lowly and despised of the world, those who count for nothing, to reduce to nothing those who are something, ²⁹so that no human being might boast before God. ³⁰It is due to him that you are in Christ Jesus, who became for us wisdom from God, as well as righteousness, sanctification, and redemption, ³¹so that, as it is written, "Whoever boasts, should boast in the Lord."

2 ¹When I came to you, brothers, proclaiming the mystery of God, I did not come with sublimity of words or of wisdom. ²For I resolved to know nothing while I was with you except Jesus

---

there to recommend them that Paul can describe them only by what they were not: not wise, not powerful, not of noble birth. But now they, too, are signs of God's power, with Christ the crucified one as the source of their power. God did not choose them according to the standards of the world. God's wisdom does not correlate, nor has it ever correlated (see Deut 7:7), with the social hierarchy established by humans. It defies human categories, demolishes human standards, and inverts human hierarchies. Now the wise are shamed. The nobodies are chosen by God to undo the somebodies, to reduce to nothing the world's standards, which are incapable of comprehending God's wisdom.

In God's choice of the Corinthians, God reveals an authority to act in a way that is independent of the world and what it thinks or how it judges things ought to be. As a result, no human being has any grounds for boasting. Self-satisfaction and arrogance are eliminated, because everyone obtains grace and salvation in the exact same way. No one has an upper hand, a more superior way or insight into God's wisdom, a higher status meriting a more privileged place within God's plan of salvation. There is only one way to know God and God's salvation: the paradox of the cross, which is God's wisdom and power. Thus competition and boasting and the resultant divisions in the community are excluded.

Paul appropriates words from Jeremiah 9:23 to conclude this subsection. Within the context of this letter, these words constitute a radical challenge to the Corinthians to let go of their boasting in human words of wisdom and human categories and begin to live out their dependence on God's grace, the source of their salvation.

2:1-5 The preaching of Paul

Since the content of the gospel message is Jesus Christ and him crucified, when Paul came to Corinth he deliberately put aside grandiose

Christ, and him crucified. ³I came to you in weakness and fear and much trembling, ⁴and my message and my proclamation were not with persuasive [words of] wisdom, but with a demonstration of spirit and power, ⁵so that your faith might rest not on human wisdom but on the power of God.

---

speech and the use of powerful rhetorical strategies to persuade the Corinthians of this mystery. Considering that the idea of Christ crucified, source of salvation and the very revelation of God's wisdom and power, was (and still is!) such a hard sell, one would think that Paul would have pulled out all his rhetorical stops to convince the Corinthians of the truth of this message. Instead he comes in "weakness and fear and much trembling" (v. 3) and speaks his message and proclamation without persuasive words of wisdom. Paul's emphatic "my" message and "my" proclamation" (v. 4) is apparently intended to distinguish himself from skilled orators and their message.

Why Paul voluntarily puts himself at such apparent rhetorical disadvantage becomes clear in verses 4-5. True understanding of God's wisdom can never come through human wisdom, which it transcends, nor through mere human articulation, which it eludes. It comes only through the power of the Spirit. Ironically, despite his apparent rhetorical disadvantage, Paul is the most advantaged because his proclamation is powered by the Spirit (v. 4), who brings about faith that rests, appropriately, on God's power.

Paul's lack of rhetorical prowess, like the Corinthians' lack of social status, illustrates again the paradoxical nature of God's wisdom, which defies human reason and subverts human standards of judgment. As God's grace does not take account of social standing, neither does it rely on the persuasive ability of the messenger and words of human wisdom for its actualization in the life of the believer. The implications for the Corinthians are clear: attachment to rhetorically skilled ministers and captivation with their hollow human wisdom leads only to vain boasting and division.

The wisdom of the mature (2:6–3:4)

Paul clears up misconceptions about wisdom, its attainment, and what constitutes true spiritual maturity (2:6-16). Unfortunately, the Corinthians who have received the Spirit persist in their immaturity, running after wisdom that sounds reasonable and is persuasively presented. As long as they persist on this course, they cannot benefit from the spiritual instruction and true wisdom that Paul is capable of imparting (3:1-4).

The True Wisdom. [6]Yet we do speak a wisdom to those who are mature, but not a wisdom of this age, nor of the rulers of this age who are passing away. [7]Rather, we speak God's wisdom, mysterious, hidden, which God predetermined before the ages for our glory, [8]and which none of the rulers of this age knew; for if they had known it, they would not have crucified the Lord of glory. [9]But as it is written:

"What eye has not seen, and ear has not heard,
and what has not entered the human heart,
what God has prepared for those who love him,"

[10]this God has revealed to us through the Spirit.

For the Spirit scrutinizes everything, even the depths of God. [11]Among human beings, who knows what pertains to a person except the spirit of the person that is within? Similarly, no one knows what pertains to God except the Spirit of God. [12]We have not received the spirit of the world but the Spirit that is from God, so that we may understand the things freely given us by God. [13]And we speak about them not with words taught by human wisdom, but with words taught by the Spirit, describing spiritual realities in spiritual terms.

2:6-16 True wisdom

In an apparent reversal of what he has just stated, Paul announces that he actually does speak a wisdom to the mature. Paul's about-face has so baffled interpreters that some regarded this subunit as originally not part of the letter. Others read it as an indication of Paul's inconsistency and insincerity. Many now read Paul's about-face as intentional irony, to wit: You want wisdom! I have wisdom for the mature. Then, having set up the spiritual snobs in the community for his esoteric message, Paul dismisses them as total infants, too stupid and immature to attain to such wisdom! Whether Paul's intention was to humiliate, as suggested by this view, is not altogether certain.

What we learn from the text is that here Paul deals with wisdom and spiritual maturity. These were of great importance not only to this community but also to Paul. However, Paul meant something radically different by these terms. Here he reconsiders both terms in light of the gospel in order to instruct the community concerning true wisdom and how it is attained, to deal with divisions caused by the spiritually enlightened, and ultimately to advance his argument for unity.

Paul begins by affirming that he does preach a wisdom, something that he has overtly claimed from the outset of this letter (1:17-18). However, this wisdom differs from that to which the Corinthians aspire. A variety of religious and philosophical currents had made their way to Corinth, but Paul does not specify the type or content of the wisdom being pursued by some

¹⁴Now the natural person does not accept what pertains to the Spirit of God, for to him it is foolishness, and he cannot understand it, because it is judged spiritually. ¹⁵The spiritual person, however, can judge everything but is not subject to judgment by anyone.

¹⁶For "who has known the mind of ▶ the Lord, so as to counsel him?" But we have the mind of Christ.

3 ¹My brothers, I could not talk to you as spiritual people, but as fleshly people, as infants in Christ. ²I fed you milk, not solid food, because you were

in the community. He simply associates it with the "wisdom of this age" (2:6), which is opposed to God's secret and hidden wisdom. The rulers of this age, operating with its wisdom, are incapable of penetrating God's wisdom; otherwise they could never have crucified the Lord of glory. The fact that they did simply illustrates that the pursuit of human wisdom leads to utter ignorance, not spiritual insight. Corinthian Christians who pursue the wisdom of this age through human reason are likewise incapable of penetrating God's wisdom, remain unenlightened, and are spiritually immature, despite their claims to the contrary.

The true wisdom to be pursued, which brings knowledge and enlightenment, is beyond what the human mind and heart can conceive and hence unattainable through human reason. It is knowable, as Paul already stated at 2:4, only through the agency of the Spirit. Paul supports his point by a commonsense argument based on human experience. The Corinthians would no doubt agree with him that one's inner workings are really scrutinized and known only by one's self. Arguing by analogy, Paul says, so it is with God. God's own Spirit scrutinizes the depths of God. Whoever would apprehend God's wisdom must be in touch with the Spirit of God and equipped with the categories and language of spiritual realities, because this is what the Spirit reveals. Paul and the Corinthians have received the Spirit of God. They are spiritual and equipped to speak of and understand God's wisdom in Spirit-taught language. Once this wisdom, summed up in the message of the cross, is understood, the criteria by which humans judge are radically changed.

3:1-4 Continued Corinthian immaturity

Paul now explains that he could not impart to the Corinthians the spiritual knowledge and insight they so desired. This was not due to any inability on his part or to any innate lack on the Corinthians' part. They had received the Spirit. They should have been able to handle Spirit-taught words, understand spiritual realities, and live as mature persons, that is, spiritual persons. But they were acting in a "fleshly" way, that is, contrary

unable to take it. Indeed, you are still not able, even now, [3]for you are still of the flesh. While there is jealousy and rivalry among you, are you not of the flesh, and behaving in an ordinary human way? [4]Whenever someone says, "I belong to Paul," and another, "I belong to Apollos," are you not merely human?

The Role of God's Ministers. [5]What is Apollos, after all, and what is Paul? Ministers through whom you became believers, just as the Lord assigned each one. [6]I planted, Apollos watered, but God caused the growth. [7]Therefore, neither the one who plants nor the one who waters is anything, but only God, who causes the growth. [8]The one who plants and the one who waters are equal, and each will receive wages in proportion to his labor. [9]For we are God's co-workers; you are God's field, God's building.

to the Spirit who unifies, still judging according to human criteria, as demonstrated by their unity-destroying behavior. While they persisted in jealousy and rivalries, they were showing themselves to be all too human. Viewed from a spiritual angle, they were still spiritual infants, unable to absorb the mysterious wisdom of the cross, the solid food reserved for spiritual adults. They had not been ready for solid food in the past, and their current wrangling over wisdom and wisdom teachers and superior status proves that they are still not ready!

The community and its leaders (3:5-23)

Paul's next step in his argument for unity deals with misunderstandings revolving around the role of community leaders. Their distinctive tasks are complementary (3:5-9); indeed, every member of the community whose foundation is Christ must contribute to its unity and holiness, in view of which one will be judged (3:10-17). Since all belongs to God in Christ, only God's wisdom revealed in Christ counts (3:18-23).

3:5-9 Paul and Apollos: co-workers in God's field

The opening rhetorical question underscores the absurdity of the partisanship that has grown up around certain ministers. Paul and Apollos are mere farm hands, working at different but equal tasks in God's field, the community, whose growth depends on God alone. The insignificance of ministers, implied in the rhetorical question, is reinforced through this metaphor and serves to warn the Corinthians against attaching too much importance to any one minister. Moreover, since, as the metaphor implies, ministers work for the same boss and undertake complementary tasks directed to the same goal, to oppose one minister to the other is to undermine God's own work.

¹⁰According to the grace of God given to me, like a wise master builder I laid a foundation, and another is building upon it. But each one must be careful how he builds upon it, ¹¹for no one can lay a foundation other than the one that is there, namely, Jesus Christ. ¹²If anyone builds on this foundation with gold, silver, precious stones, wood, hay, or straw, ¹³the work of each will come to light, for the Day will disclose it. It will be revealed with fire, and the fire [itself] will test the quality of each one's work. ¹⁴If the work stands that someone built upon the foundation, that person will receive a wage. ¹⁵But if someone's work is burned up, that one will suffer loss; the person will be saved, but only as through fire. ¹⁶Do you not know that you are the temple of God, and that the Spirit of God dwells in you? ¹⁷If anyone destroys God's temple, God will destroy that person; for the temple of God, which you are, is holy.

3:10-17 Everyone's work will be fire-tested

At the end of 3:9, Paul changes metaphors, describing the community as God's building, and now advances his argument employing construction imagery (3:10-15). Paul, the wise master builder, laid the foundation for God's building, Jesus Christ. As a foundation determines the contours and shape of the concrete structure arising from it, so must the community of believers, whose oneness is underscored by the term "building," be determined by its foundation, Christ. Each member builds up from this one foundation and must take care that the contribution made is consistent with it and ordered to the building's unity. Paul directs this warning not to Apollos and himself but to the Corinthians. They can build on the foundation with precious stones, or with perishable materials such as wood or hay, by which Paul means the fleeting and fatuous stuff of human wisdom. The latter will not stand the fire test, that is, the day of judgment, when retribution or salvation will be awarded in light of one's work.

Indeed, if anyone destroys this building, now further qualified as God's temple (3:16-17), God will destroy that person. Paul uses the Greek term *naos*, translated "temple," which actually referred to a particular place within the temple—the inner sanctuary where God's holiness dwelt. Thus the Corinthian community, *corporately as a community*, indwelt by God's own Spirit, is now the living locus of God's holiness. As a result, each member's behavior must be oriented from and toward the community's holiness.

3:18-23 All belong to God in Christ

In concluding this subunit of argumentation, Paul once again takes up the themes of wisdom and folly and very bluntly addresses the Corinthians.

¹⁸Let no one deceive himself. If any one among you considers himself wise in this age, let him become a fool so as to become wise. ¹⁹For the wisdom of this world is foolishness in the eyes of God, for it is written:

"He catches the wise in their own ruses,"

²⁰and again:

"The Lord knows the thoughts of the wise, that they are vain."

²¹So let no one boast about human beings, for everything belongs to you, ²²Paul or Apollos or Cephas, or the world or life or death, or the present or the future: all belong to you, ²³and you to Christ, and Christ to God.

The world's wisdom is mere craftiness, a human construct of hollow notions, two facts attested by the Scriptures Paul cites (Job 5:13 and Ps 94:11).

If you think yourself wise in view of that standard, your self-perception is actually self-deception! Give up that standard! Accept and submit to the inverted order that is paradoxically God's wisdom, epitomized in the cross, and then, though the world considers you a fool, paradoxically, you will be truly wise!

Within this paradoxical perspective, the futility of exalting any one minister over another and divisive boasting over human wisdom becomes apparent. Every minister plays an equal and complementary part in unfolding God's plan, and all ministers are at the service of the Corinthians, who together have "everything" (3:21). Here Paul cites a popular maxim of his day summarizing all the privileges believed to accrue to the ideal wise person, a completely self-sufficient person of superior status who was beyond the petty rules and regulations that applied to the less enlightened.

In contradistinction to this privilege and autonomy, Paul reminds the Corinthians that together, as a community, they are co-sharers and co-inheritors of all things in and with Christ. As such, no one can use his or her freedom and privilege for individual self-promotion and boasting, or toward whatever destroys the unity of the community in Christ through which these privileges exist. Moreover, the Corinthian cowmmunity ultimately stands in and through Christ in direct and subordinate relationship *to God* (3:23). The Corinthians must ultimately live in faithful obedience to God and answer to God, not Paul or Apollos or Cephas, not even Christ, but God who holds all together and judges all according to the wisdom made manifest in the cross.

Cross-wisdom: the ultimate critique (4:1-21)

In this final step of his argument, Paul returns to the role of ministers and appropriates another set of metaphors that stress the subordinate role

◀ **4** ¹Thus should one regard us: as servants of Christ and stewards of the mysteries of God. ²Now it is of course required of stewards that they be found trustworthy. ³It does not concern me in the least that I be judged by you or any human tribunal; I do not even pass judgment on myself; ⁴I am not conscious of anything against me, but I do not thereby stand acquitted; the one who judges me is the Lord. ⁵Therefore, do ▶ not make any judgment before the appointed time, until the Lord comes, for he will bring to light what is hidden in darkness and will manifest the motives of our hearts, and then everyone will receive praise from God.

of ministers and the singular character upon which they are to be judged—trustworthiness (4:1-5). This is followed by a stinging critique of the Corinthian community in light of cross-wisdom. Judged by the criterion of the cross, their lives are shown to be a repudiation of God's counter-order wisdom (4:6-13). Paul's highlighting of their failure to live lives transformed by the gospel of the cross is intended to restore a sense of realism to the situation so that the Corinthians can go forward to restore the unity of the community.

4:1-5 Ministers are required to be trustworthy

Changing metaphors, Paul now describes ministers as "servants" and "stewards," persons who work under the authority of a master and are accountable to the master's standards. The singular requirement to which they are held is trustworthiness, that is, they must be faithful to the proclamation of Christ crucified, God's wisdom. In context, this statement should probably be understood as an implicit critique of the standard of judgment applied to ministers by the Corinthians. They were impressed by parcels of wisdom and grandiose speech, the wrong criteria applied by some Corinthians, who had wrongly arrogated to themselves the right to judge ministers. It was not that ministers were beyond judgment. But they were accountable to God, not the Corinthians.

Even the fact that Paul is the founding apostle of this community in no way invests the Corinthians with any particular right to judge him or any other minister of God. The right to judge and the criterion for judgment are God's alone. So much so is this the exclusive prerogative of God that Paul, who is spiritually mature, does not even bother to judge himself. (How much less should the spiritually immature judge others?) Besides, Paul knew that even were he to find himself beyond reproach by the light of his own conscience, it was not one's conscience but only God who is the ultimate arbiter of truth and under whose eschatological judgment everyone

Paul's Life as Pattern. [6]I have applied these things to myself and Apollos for your benefit, brothers, so that you may learn from us not to go beyond what is written, so that none of you will be inflated with pride in favor of one person over against another. [7]Who confers distinction upon you? What do you possess that you have not received? But if you have received it, why are you boasting as if you did not receive it? [8]You are already satisfied; you have already grown rich; you have become kings without us! Indeed, I wish that you had become kings, so that we also might become kings with you.

[9]For as I see it, God has exhibited us apostles as the last of all, like people

must pass. God's future judgment is the only thing that counts, and God's verdict depends not only on what one does in the present but also on one's hidden motivations!

4:6-13 Cross-wisdom: the ultimate critique

Paul now explains that he has discussed these things by way of reference to Apollos and himself in order to teach the Corinthians a beneficial lesson about how they are to act among themselves. Through the example of Apollos and himself, Paul was able to underscore the cooperative and complementary character of ministry. Neither he nor Apollos does anything that is self-serving; rather, both work toward the same common purpose. Neither is a Hellenistic wise man to be made a rallying point for partisan allegiance; rather, both are servants and stewards whose allegiance is directed to God.

The Corinthians are to learn from this "not to go beyond what is written" (4:6). The meaning of "what is written" is a matter of speculation. It could refer to the Scriptures in general, to the gospel of the cross, to all Paul has thus far written in this letter, or to the specific sections of Scripture he has so far cited. The whole phrase, "not to go beyond what is written," could also be Paul's adaptation of an adage connoting something like "stick to the guidelines."

Whatever the case, Paul's clear intention is stated in the rest of verse 6, namely, that they desist from the divisive behavior caused by their pitting one leader against another. This is accompanied by prideful boasting ("inflated with pride," literally being "puffed up"). As the image suggests, they are "puffed up" by empty wind, mere pretentiousness but no substance.

Paul's three questions in verse 7 serve as a reality check. There is nothing different or special about the Corinthians. Anything they have is a gift, made possible by the cross of Christ. Yet, rather than living an existence consonant with that reality, characterized by the paradoxical wisdom of

sentenced to death, since we have become a spectacle to the world, to angels and human beings alike. [10]We are fools on Christ's account, but you are wise in Christ; we are weak, but you are strong; you are held in honor, but we in disrepute. [11]To this very hour we go hungry and thirsty, we are poorly clad and roughly treated, we wander about homeless [12]and we toil, working with our own hands. When ridiculed, we bless; when persecuted, we endure; [13]when slandered, we respond gently. We have become like the world's rubbish, the scum of all, to this very moment.

[14]I am writing you this not to shame you, but to admonish you as my beloved children. [15]Even if you should have countless guides to Christ, yet you do not have many fathers, for I became your father in Christ Jesus through the gospel. [16]Therefore, I urge you, be imita-

the cross, the Corinthians live another triumphant existence guided and evaluated in view of other standards. They claim to have it all, to be rich in spiritual-intellectual assets, and to have been already empowered to reign. In philosophical circles, especially among the Stoics, to be rich and to reign were applied to intellectual-spiritual status and represented the prerogatives of the ideal wise person. Apparently, the Corinthians were still aspiring to the values of their world, mixing up the goals of gospel living with society's goals and using the standard of judgment applied by society to measure their own wisdom and spiritual maturity.

In his critique of the Corinthians, Paul transposes the whole problem to a theological key. In that key the problem is presented as rooted in a premature arrogating of the full privileges of end-time living and the status of the spiritually perfect by the community. Paul goes on to contrast the Corinthians' grandstanding with the lot of apostles with purposeful irony aimed at Corinthian pretentiousness. Apostles are weak and considered fools; their lives are characterized by hardship and deprivation. So low is their social status that Paul likens apostles to "the world's rubbish, the scum of all" (4:13)! All this is in contradistinction to the lot of the Corinthians, who, Paul mockingly observes, are wise, strong, and esteemed. Judged by the world's standards, apostles are nothing and the Corinthians are everything! But when each stands under the critique of the cross, all such judgments are reversed. By their vain boasting and glorying in their own achievements, the Corinthians repudiate God's wisdom and the suffering and crucified Christ in whom this wisdom was revealed. In the starkest possible terms, Paul makes it clear that true ministers, indeed every true follower of Christ, must be co-sharers not only in Christ's glory but in his sufferings and status as one rejected by the world.

tors of me. [17]For this reason I am sending you Timothy, who is my beloved and faithful son in the Lord; he will remind you of my ways in Christ [Jesus], just as I teach them everywhere in every church.

[18]Some have become inflated with pride, as if I were not coming to you.

[19]But I will come to you soon, if the Lord is willing, and I shall ascertain not the talk of these inflated people but their power. [20]For the kingdom of God is not a matter of talk but of power. [21]Which do you prefer? Shall I come to you with a rod, or with love and a gentle spirit?

4:14-21 Concluding admonition

Having just taken the Corinthians down a few pegs, Paul now explains that his harsh rhetoric was not intended to shame but to admonish and refocus the perspective of the Corinthians, whom he genuinely loves. Whereas in 3:1-5 Paul referred to his relationship with the community using the maternal imagery of nourishing, here he refers to himself metaphorically as their "father" (4:15), giving expression to the intimate relationship between himself and this community engendered through his preaching of the gospel. Paul's paternal intervention and call for the community to be imitators of him (4:16) could be read as the ultimate expression of patriarchal arrogance. However, read in context, Paul's call for imitation is contingent upon his own imitation of Christ and refers to the pattern of renunciation, suffering, and servant-model type of leadership that he undertakes for the sake of the gospel. Here Paul's own *ethos* becomes a powerful appeal to the Corinthians to transform their own lives. In Paul's absence, he sends Timothy as one who will model this life pattern ("my ways in Christ Jesus," 4:17) for the community. This manner of life is not a distinct imposition on the Corinthians, but the pattern of life required of all Christians everywhere. Here again Paul reminds the Corinthians that they are no maverick community of elite spiritualists, but part of a universal fellowship.

Despite the arguments that Paul has set out in this first major unit of the letter, he is concerned that some will persist in the behavior that has been a source of division in the community. He has already made it eminently clear that God's wisdom and power are not compatible with human words, no matter how elegant and persuasive the articulation. Here he contrasts empty words and true power again, and if need be, Paul will come and reveal the impotence of the empty talkers.

With this final warning, Paul concludes the first major argument of this letter. Throughout this argument for unity, he has applied the scandalous and paradoxical lens of the cross to the situation of this community. Through that lens, it becomes clear that the Corinthians are still

B. Moral Disorders

◄ **5** **A Case of Incest.** [1]It is widely reported that there is immorality among you, and immorality of a kind not found even among pagans—a man living with his father's wife. [2]And you are inflated with pride. Should you not rather have been sorrowful? The one who did this deed should be expelled from your midst. [3]I, for my part,

---

dominated by the values and presuppositions of their culture. They are still searching for the human wisdom that will unlock the door to power and status, still judging people by the secular categories of prestige and success. They remain impressed by elegant words and controlled by the desire for enhanced status afforded by attachment to the best purveyor of human wisdom. The Corinthians' culturally conditioned living of the gospel had emptied the cross of Christ of its power and value and resulted in the problems that were threatening to destroy Christianity at Corinth. The restoration of the community's unity, as Paul has demonstrated, would require nothing less than the entire realigning of its values with God's countercultural cross-wisdom.

ARGUMENTS CONCERNING IMMORALITY WITHIN THE COMMUNITY AND RELATIONSHIPS WITH THOSE OUTSIDE THE COMMUNITY

1 Corinthians 5:1–6:20

Paul now takes up three ethical issues, beginning with a case of sexual immorality at 1 Corinthians 5. The logical disjuncture between the previous discussion in chapters 1–4 and its themes and this new one, focused on an individual case of sexual immorality, has contributed to the speculation that 1 Corinthians is not one unified literary composition. However, this is too radical an assessment since there are word links—for example, to boast, to judge—between 1 Corinthians 5 and the chapters that precede it. Nonetheless, it is clear that chapters 5–6 do form a distinct macro-unit, structured according to the ABA' pattern. Sexual immorality is introduced in 5:1-13 (A). Then Paul discusses Christian recourse to pagan courts in 6:1-11 (B), before again dealing with sexual immorality in 6:12-20 (A').

Why Paul introduces these three topics here can perhaps be best explained in view of their rhetorical-pedagogic function in the letter. As 1 Corinthians progresses, Paul takes up a variety of questions for which there are no black-and-white answers. Instead, the community has to consider not only the good but also the better courses of action that they as Christians must adopt in view of the well-being of the whole community.

although absent in body but present in spirit, have already, as if present, pronounced judgment on the one who has committed this deed, ⁴in the name of [our] Lord Jesus: when you have gathered together and I am with you in spirit

Multiple criteria have to be considered, and keen powers of discernment are needed to weigh the options.

A closer look at 1 Corinthians 5–6 reveals the community's incompetence to handle matters where clear-cut decisions are called for. In the face of this, here in chapters 5–6, Paul first reorders the Corinthians' focus within the fundamental boundaries of absolute good and evil as a prelude to assisting them with decisions on issues that admit of shades of gray. If the community cannot judge black-and-white cases of community-destroying behavior, how can Paul expect them to be able to discern what is best for the community?

Argument against sexual immorality (5:1-13)

In this subunit of argumentation, Paul deals with a blatant case of sexual immorality within the community. It was apparently tolerated rather than dealt with and stopped. Paul's unequivocal judgment is that the offender needs to be expelled from the community to protect its holiness. The decision to excommunicate, however, ultimately remains with the community. In this compact unit, Paul argues to persuade the Corinthians to take the prescribed action.

5:1-5 The community's failed judgment

Whatever the exact contents of the report Paul heard, he states the problem this way: "there is immorality *(porneia)* among you (plural)." This manner of articulating the problem indicates that Paul's overriding concern is with the community, which has allowed the situation to go unchecked. The Greek term *porneia* is a comprehensive term covering all forms of sexual immorality. By adding the phrase "a man living with his father's wife," Paul qualifies the immorality as incest. "Father's wife" was used to distinguish one's stepmother from one's biological mother (Lev 18:7-8).

What Paul says, literally, is that the man "is having" his stepmother, a verb normally used to indicate a sexual relationship, which, in view of the present tense, should be considered ongoing. Such a relationship, proscribed by both Jewish and Roman law, is simply wrong, even if the offender's father is dead. Thus there is no need to argue for the man's guilt. Yet, the community has failed to judge the situation for what it is—a case of rank evil in its midst—and has allowed the brother to carry on unimpugned.

with the power of the Lord Jesus, ⁵you are to deliver this man to Satan for the destruction of his flesh, so that his spirit may be saved on the day of the Lord.	⁶Your boasting is not appropriate. ▶ Do you not know that a little yeast leavens all the dough? ⁷Clear out the ▶ old yeast, so that you may become a

Not only that, they are inflated with pride either because of the relationship or perhaps despite it. Whatever the case, their haughty attitude is the real cause of Paul's consternation and the bigger issue circumscribing the problem addressed in this chapter.

Since the Corinthians have failed to judge correctly and do the obvious, Paul, who has judged correctly, outlines the action that ought to be taken. The exact punishment envisioned by him is unclear. He could be intending physical death, or physical punishment coupled with expulsion, or simply expulsion from the community. When all the data is assessed, it seems more likely that Paul intends the latter. Banished from the community, presumably the offender will come to his senses and repent. Whatever the punishment, one thing is clear: it is ultimately ordered to the benefit of the offender so that "his spirit may be saved on the day of the Lord" (v. 5). Here Paul is not deliberating with the community among possible courses of action. This is the only course possible, and it is imperative that the community carry it out.

Paul obviously realizes that commanding alone will not move the community to take action, and so he couches his call for expulsion in three distinct arguments. The first argument is introduced with his remark that such behavior is not found even among the pagans! This statement is no doubt an exaggeration. However, the exaggerated comparison between the pagans and the Corinthians functions as an appeal to their emotions (argument based on *pathos*). The community should be ashamed of itself for disregarding a common standard of decency that even pagans are capable of observing. Appeals to the emotions, especially shame, were considered among the most powerful arguments to induce a person or group to change judgments, if for no nobler reason than simply to avoid being disgraced. To the Corinthians, who lived in an honor/shame culture, saving face was of utmost importance.

5:6-8 "you are unleavened"

After dismissing the Corinthian boasting as not good, Paul proceeds to appeal to the Corinthians' reason. Using a commonsense maxim, he takes up the metaphoric language of dough and yeast and argues on analogy that the evil one's presence is corrupting and compromising the entire

fresh batch of dough, inasmuch as you are unleavened. For our paschal lamb, Christ, has been sacrificed. [8]Therefore let us celebrate the feast, not with the old yeast, the yeast of malice and wickedness, but with the unleavened bread of sincerity and truth.

[9]I wrote you in my letter not to associate with immoral people, [10]not at all referring to the immoral of this world or the greedy and robbers or idolaters; for you would then have to leave the world. [11]But I now write to you not to associate with anyone named a brother, if he is

---

community's true character of sinlessness. Since the community is sinless, it cannot at the same time have sin in its midst. This incompatibility demands that the sinner be expelled, metaphorically expressed in the command to "clear out the old yeast" (v. 7). Paul explains why sinlessness is the character of Christian existence and necessitates this cleansing in one brief phrase: "for our paschal lamb, Christ, has been sacrificed." The mention of the paschal lamb and unleavened bread recalls the rites of the Jewish Passover, which Paul symbolically interprets and transposes to a moral key. Through Christ's blood, Christians are morally cleansed, constituted holy, a condition willed by God (see 1 Thess 4:2). This is the core of Paul's reasoning and the ultimate ground of the specific command to expel the sinner. Paul concludes this section by exhorting the community to live in a manner consistent with its own sinless/holy character.

5:9-13 The community's failed judgment

Paul returns to the community's failed judgment by referring to his previous letter to the Corinthians. They had missed Paul's point. He was not prohibiting social interaction with the immoral of the society at large but, as he now clarifies, with anyone calling himself a brother who perpetrated any of the vices Paul now lists in verse 11. The introduction of the list of vices allows Paul to class the offending brother with egregious sinners. By doing so, he again appeals to the community's emotions, to elicit a sense of abhorrence for and alienation from "such a person," which should move them to judge and expel him. The vice-list makes clear that there is no double-standard. A vice-doer who is a brother is not a brother but a sinner. Here Paul draws the line not between Christians and pagans but between Christians and pseudo-Christians. There can be no social contact with the latter!

In conclusion, Paul disclaims any obligation to judge those outside the community. As outsiders, they cannot corrupt the community's holiness. But those within can, and so he reminds the community of its obligation to judge the sinners within the community and, as this case warrants, "purge the evil person from your midst" (v. 13). This paraphrase of a formula re-

immoral, greedy, an idolater, a slanderer, a drunkard, or a robber, not even to eat with such a person. ¹²For why should I be judging outsiders? Is it not your business to judge those within? ¹³God will judge those outside. "Purge the evil person from your midst."

6 **Lawsuits before Unbelievers.** ¹How can any one of you with a case against another dare to bring it to the unjust for judgment instead of to the holy ones? ²Do you not know that the holy ones will judge the world? If the world is to be judged by you, are you

---

peated in Deuteronomy (e.g., Deut 17:7; 19:19; 21:21; 22:21, 22, 24) echoes the punishment prescribed in the Torah for egregious sins and evokes Jewish abhorrence for sexual sin, especially incest, considered the characteristic practice of pagans (Lev 18:1-3).

Thus, by Jewish lights and by the standards of common decency of society at large, incest is intolerable. Christians cannot ignore these standards as a baseline for their own behavior. However, what ultimately must guide Christian behavior is the person of Christ and the event of his death, on account of which the community's corporate identity as sanctified is established. This ecclesial identity is linked to ethical behavior, which must be ordered to safeguarding the sanctified life of the community.

Since Paul does not discuss the reasons why the offending brother undertook this relationship or why the community tolerated his presence, speculation abounds concerning their motives. In view of the discussion in 1 Corinthians 1–4, where it appears that some had arrogated to themselves the status and prerogatives of the ideal wise person, perhaps their complacent disregard for this violation of the standards of common decency, or even boasting about it, was intended to demonstrate that they had arrived at a state of perfection that allowed them to transcend all the conventions to which the unenlightened were obligated. If so, then here again some community members confused the standard of human wisdom and the exercise of privileges reserved for the world's wise with the standards that must guide Christians and the privilege of sanctified life in Christ, which enjoins on each member the obligation to live as a sanctified member of a sanctified community.

Argument against recourse to pagan courts (6:1-11)

Having brought up the need for the community to exercise jurisdiction for internal matters, Paul leaves aside the issue of sexual immorality and excoriates the community for abdicating this responsibility and allowing the adjudication of internal community issues to take place before pagan

unqualified for the lowest law courts? ³Do you not know that we will judge angels? Then why not everyday matters? ⁴If, therefore, you have courts for everyday matters, do you seat as judges people of no standing in the church? ⁵I say this to shame you. Can it be that there is not one among you wise enough

---

courts. Paul does not say how he learned about this situation However, he argues against such recourse on two grounds. First, Christians are competent to adjudicate their own disputes (6:1-6), and second, Christians ought not to have such disputes requiring litigation in the first place (6:7-8). In concluding, Paul reminds the community that certain forms of behavior are simply incompatible with its new corporate ecclesial identity (6:9-11).

6:1-6 Competence to judge

Paul first expresses his shock in a rhetorical question, one of the nine such questions that he will use in this subunit to bring his argument forward. Explicit in this first question is the community's failure to carry out its responsibility by going before the "unjust" (v. 1). Although the Roman court system was known for its corruption and favoring of the well-to-do in its exploitation of the poor, in context "unjust" is probably to be taken less as a moral evaluation and more as a term to distinguish those outside from those inside the communion of the holy ones.

In the next two rhetorical questions Paul reminds the community of its judicial prerogatives. The belief that the holy ones would judge the world was rooted in Jewish apocalyptic eschatology, which envisioned the role of judgment as one of the prerogatives of God's elect (Dan 7:21-22). Many later Jewish writings also anticipate the participation of the holy ones in the final judgment (e.g., Wis 3:7-8; Sir 4:11).

Paul goes further in his next question to suggest that they will even judge the angels (v. 3), presumably the fallen ones, who were expected to undergo judgment (2 Pet 2:4). By reminding them of their prerogatives as holy ones, Paul builds an argument from greater to lesser to point up both the absurdity and inappropriateness of recourse to pagan courts. If in their glorious eschatological future they will sit in judgment on the world (including, obviously, the ones to whom they now hand over their judgments) and even angels, how much more so should they be capable of handling minor and ordinary everyday cases in the present! Paul does not specify what type of cases, but his choice of words underscores their inconsequential nature.

Why, then, Paul continues, do you elevate to the role of judges "people of no standing in the church"? (v. 4). It would be bad enough had the com-

to be able to settle a case between brothers? ⁶But rather brother goes to court against brother, and that before unbelievers?

⁷Now indeed [then] it is, in any case, a failure on your part that you have lawsuits against one another. Why not rather put up with injustice? Why not rather let yourselves be cheated? ⁸Instead, you inflict injustice and cheat, and this to brothers. ⁹Do you not know that the unjust will not inherit the kingdom

---

munity simply failed to perform its duty, but it has actually ceded its privilege to a secular system and its standards of judgment. This act of submission to that system indicates that the community is still tied to the social conventions of the world and has yet to redirect its total allegiance to the community of faith. Paul's explicit intent to shame the community should at least awaken their concern to save face, and indeed they have much to be ashamed about. The need to take inconsequential cases before unbelievers seems to point up the community's deficiency when it comes to judiciousness, despite all the claims to be truly wise!

6:7-8 Renouncing litigation

With two more questions Paul advances his argument in another direction. Community members should renounce their right to litigate to the detriment of other community members and, instead, endure injustice and defrauding. This idea had great currency among philosophers who held that a truly wise person was above injury or insult. Seeking redress would simply negate this claim, and the wise one would show himself or herself to be no better than anyone else! Paul may be playing off Corinthian arrogance at this point.

Beyond that, it is important to recognize that what Paul says here is quite consistent with what he says elsewhere about how Christians must comport themselves (Rom 12:17) and, though unstated, is obviously rooted in the example of Christ, who endured injustice without seeking redress. But not only have the Corinthians paraded their problems before the unjust, but in the very act of doing this they have become perpetrators of injustice and cheating against their own family. The distinction between the world and the family of faith has been blurred.

6:9-11 Final warning

Paul's final rhetorical question insinuates that the glorious eschatological destiny that awaits the Corinthians will not be had simply by waiting. In fact, if they do wrong they risk sharing the lot of those who will not inherit the kingdom. Paul again cautions them against self-deception (v. 9;

of God? Do not be deceived; neither fornicators nor idolaters nor adulterers nor boy prostitutes nor sodomites [10]nor thieves nor the greedy nor drunkards nor slanderers nor robbers will inherit the kingdom of God. [11]That is what some of you used to be; but now you have had yourselves washed, you were sanctified, you were justified in the name of the Lord Jesus Christ and in the Spirit of our God.

Sexual Immorality. [12]"Everything is lawful for me," but not everything is beneficial. "Everything is lawful for me," but I will not let myself be dominated by anything. [13]"Food for the stomach and the stomach for food," but God will do away with both the one and the other. The body, however, is not for immorality, but for the Lord, and the Lord is for the body; [14]God raised the Lord and will also raise us by his power.

---

cf. 3:18) and lists the vices that characterized some of their former lives as pagans. They have to continuously renounce all such behavior and live as those who are washed, sanctified, and justified. Together these three terms express the fullness of the transformation that has taken place in the lives of believers, who are now in Christ and made one and holy by the indwelling of the Spirit of God. In this one family of believers, brothers cannot go against brothers, nor can the holy ones mix with the unjust.

Argument against sexual immorality (6:12-20)

Paul now returns to the topic of sexual immorality. However, here there is no indication that the type of *porneia* under discussion, that is, extramarital sexual unions, perhaps with prostitutes, represents the actual behavior of some community members or simply behavior that could hypothetically result from the exercise of freedom understood apart from a theological context. In the form of a dialogue between himself and an imaginary dialogue partner, Paul engages and corrects the Corinthians' errant thinking and then, through a series of rhetorical questions, moves his argument against fornication forward. He frames this entire discussion within two important parameters: Christians are free (6:12), but they belong to God (6:19).

6:12-14 Everything is lawful for me

The phrase "Everything is lawful for me," marked off in the biblical text with quotation marks, is a Corinthian principle or slogan cited by Paul. Paul had indeed preached freedom from sin as one of the hallmarks of new Christian existence (1 Cor 6:11; Gal 5:1). However, once again it appears that the Corinthians had interpreted Paul's freedom teaching apart from its theological and ethical significance and in accord with societal ideas and categories. According to the philosophers, freedom was the authority to

43

◄ ¹⁵Do you not know that your bodies are members of Christ? Shall I then take Christ's members and make them the members of a prostitute? Of course not! ¹⁶[Or] do you not know that anyone who joins himself to a prostitute

---

act on one's own, the quintessential right and privilege of the ideal wise person. Especially among the Stoics, it was believed that this freedom was manifested in one's acting according to nature.

After qualifying the use of freedom in view of what is beneficial, presumably for the whole community, and the need for self-control, Paul moves closer to the heart of the matter in verse 13, where he quotes another Corinthian slogan: "Food for the stomach and the stomach for food." In other words, as the Corinthians saw it, the sating of the stomach was considered a natural biological necessity. Moreover, they obviously held that no moral value could be attached to acts of natural biological necessity, because the body was meant ultimately for destruction, which proved its moral insignificance.

The Corinthians presumably transferred this way of thinking to sex to argue that it was merely another natural biological necessity, no more than the functioning of morally insignificant parts of a morally insignificant body. The blatant disregard for the body manifested in such thinking accorded very well with the view of the body expressed by the philosophers, especially the Stoics, who looked forward to death as the release of the soul from one's paltry body.

Here Paul's concern is that the inferior status accorded to the body could lead to fornication, and so he insists that the body is not meant for immorality but for the Lord! Moreover, against nature which destroys, Paul establishes the power and purpose of God, who raised Jesus and who will raise us. That future glorious eschatological destiny imbues the body with moral value and impinges on what one does in the body in the present. The reality of the resurrection, which grounds Paul's argument here, anticipates his fuller argument for the resurrection in chapter 15.

6:15-20 You are not your own

Through a series of rhetorical questions, Paul now adds to this argument, rooted in the resurrection destiny of the body, an argument rooted in the believers' union with Christ and another rooted in a consideration of the body as the temple of the holy Spirit. Picking up on his statement that the body is for the Lord, Paul now reminds the Corinthians of their union with Christ, a union so intimate that Paul uses the imagery of sexual union

becomes one body with her? For "the two," it says, "will become one flesh." [17]But whoever is joined to the Lord becomes one spirit with him. [18]Avoid immorality. Every other sin a person commits is outside the body, but the immoral person sins against his own body. [19]Do you not know that your body is a temple of the holy Spirit within you, whom you have from God, and that you are not your own? [20]For you have been purchased at a price. Therefore glorify God in your body.

---

to describe it. As unthinkable as it would be for a man or woman to take his or her body, which is one with his or her spouse, and unite it sexually to another, so also is it unthinkable for a Christian who is one with Christ ("one spirit with him," v. 17) to form another union. This union of believers with Christ in one holy body precludes immoral unions between a believer and a prostitute, which constitute a defilement of the whole Christian community. Thus Paul commands believers to flee immorality!

Before discussing the sanctifying role of the Spirit, Paul counters another Corinthian argument to the effect that the physical body has nothing to do with sin. This squares well with the Corinthian argument that bodily actions were deemed to have no moral significance, which Paul has already countered. It may also underscore how much the Corinthians' thinking was influenced by the philosophers of the day, since the argument that the body has nothing to do with sin fits very well with the Stoic idea that sin is not in the performance of any particular external act but is a matter of interior intention. Paul does not recognize this dichotomy between act and intention. His reaction is clear: a fornicator defiles not only the community but himself or herself, who is indwelt by the Spirit.

Here Paul returns to the image of the temple of God. At 3:16-17 Paul spoke of the Spirit who indwells the community as a whole, and now he applies this metaphor to every member individually. As the entire community must safeguard its holiness, so must each individual believer, whose body is no longer his or her own to use at will but is the sacred place of God's dwelling. Thus the Corinthians, corporately and individually, are free, but they are not totally autonomous. God has a claim on them. They have been bought at the price of Christ's death.

For Corinthians, exposed to the buying and selling of slaves in the marketplace, the implications of this metaphoric language would have been clear. They now belong to God and stand under God's authority and will. To accept the offer of freedom that comes through Christ is to stand in a new relationship, to accept a new bondage with ethical implications. Therefore the freedom exercised by those in Christ is never absolute freedom

III. Answers to the Corinthians' Questions

A. Marriage and Virginity

7 Advice to the Married. [1]Now in regard to the matters about which you wrote: "It is a good thing for a man not to touch a woman," [2]but because of cases of immorality every man should have his own wife, and every woman her own husband. [3]The husband should fulfill his duty toward his wife, and likewise the wife toward her husband. [4]A wife does not have authority over her

---

but freedom exercised within the parameters of belonging to God in Christ and ordered to God's glory. It was this relationally circumscribed and theologically inflected understanding of freedom that the wise ones at Corinth apparently failed to perceive.

In both 1 Corinthians 5 and here in 6:12-20, Paul does not treat sexual morality as a purely individual matter of choice, with only individual consequences. Since the community forms one sanctified whole, the immorality of one member can damage the sanctified life of the whole body. The community as a whole must be vigilant about this holiness and take responsibility to cleanse itself from whatever mars that holiness (5:1-13). The individual, too, must be vigilant for the life of the whole and avoid through his or her own exercise of freedom any defilement of the community's sanctified life (6:12-20). By the holiness of its life, manifested at the level of moral existence, the community of believers must glorify God and distinguish itself from the world. To bring community issues before outsiders blurs the distinction between this holy community and the world, dishonors God, and shows the community to be incapable of the reconciling love demanded by the cross-wisdom that must guide this community (6:1-11).

CONCERNING MARRIAGE AND SEXUAL RELATIONS

1 Corinthians 7:1-40

Having just discussed immoral sexual relations outside marriage, Paul now turns to discuss the question of sexual relations within marriage, offering advice to the married as well as to the unmarried and widows (7:1-16). This is followed by an apparent digression relating to social status (7:17-24). Then Paul redirects himself to virgins, widows, and married women.

It is important to remember when reading 1 Corinthians 7 that Paul is not writing a systematic treatise on marriage but is responding to questions posed by the community (see 7:1). His answers are conditioned by his belief that the community is living in the last days of the end-time and that the

The rostrum (bema) at which Paul defended himself before the Roman proconsul Gallio

own body, but rather her husband, and similarly a husband does not have authority over his own body, but rather his

wife. [5]Do not deprive each other, except perhaps by mutual consent for a time, to be free for prayer, but then return to one

---

Lord's second coming is quickly approaching. Unfortunately, Paul's advice here has been mistakenly read as a devaluation of marriage and human sexuality and expressive of an overall contempt of women. Once one recognizes the occasional nature of Paul's responses and the eschatological urgency that conditioned them, it is quite clear that this presentation of Paul and his teaching is a distortion in service of a negative agenda about marriage, sexuality, and women that was not Paul's.

To appreciate Paul's discussion, some information about currents of discussion in Paul's day will be helpful. Among the philosophers, the relative merits of marriage were a regular topic of discussion, and written record reveals their ambivalence about it. While it was conceded that marriage was good for the ordinary citizen and promoted the well-being of society, some argued that marriage, with all its obligations and strains, was ill-suited to the ideal wise one and hindered the pursuit of wisdom. For such a one, it was argued, to remain unmarried, which did not imply sexually chaste, was a better option.

Some of the Corinthians who fancied themselves as spiritually enlightened seem to have taken up the lines of this debate with regard to their own situation. Some may have thought that sexual asceticism would further their pursuit of wisdom and establish their superior status as those dedicated to spiritual matters rather than the mundane preoccupations of the less enlightened. In any event, the community directs the matter to Paul, who does not have black-and-white answers to these issues. Rather, he considers with the community what is preferable, balancing his answers between what is practically doable in the particular situation in which members find themselves and the urgency of the present eschatological situation.

7:1-16 Advice to the married, unmarried, and widows

Paul begins by citing another Corinthian slogan. This one is concerned with "touch[ing] a woman," a euphemism for sexual intercourse. Apparently some proposed the renunciation of sexual relations within marriage in view of their new spiritual status or even the renunciation of marriage and sex altogether in preference for celibacy. While Paul clearly prefers the latter, he clarifies that within the married state, one cannot renounce

another, so that Satan may not tempt you through your lack of self-control. ⁶This I say by way of concession, however, not as a command. ⁷Indeed, I wish everyone to be as I am, but each has a particular gift from God, one of one kind and one of another.

⁸Now to the unmarried and to widows, I say: It is a good thing for them to remain as they are, as I do, ⁹but if they cannot exercise self-control they should marry, for it is better to marry than to be on fire. ¹⁰To the married, however, I give this instruction (not I, but the Lord): A wife should not separate from her husband ¹¹—and if she does separate she must either remain single or become reconciled to her husband—and a husband should not divorce his wife.

¹²To the rest I say (not the Lord): If any brother has a wife who is an unbeliever, and she is willing to go on living with him, he should not divorce her; ¹³and if any woman has a husband who

---

sexual activity in order to be more spiritual, because this misplaced asceticism could wind up leading to immorality! Far from denouncing erotic pleasure within marriage, Paul urges married people to do what is proper to married people. Marriage enjoins on both man and woman equal obligation and equal rights over their sexual relationship. Neither can unilaterally withdraw from these obligations except for prayer, an option afforded by Jewish law, which Paul seems to have in mind here. But even this must be by mutual agreement. It is possible that some at Corinth were appealing to Paul's own celibacy to justify sexual asceticism. However, he makes it clear that celibacy is a gift from God. Since celibacy cannot be self-imposed or externally imposed, for Paul it follows that not marrying is possible and preferable only if one is gifted with celibacy by God.

To the unmarried and widows, Paul does cite his own celibacy as a model to be followed, although he is well aware that the sexual drive may prove to be too much for some, in which case he counsels marriage. To the married, Paul specifies that he repeats the Lord's own instruction, that is, the prohibition of divorce. Though Paul cautions both men and women against divorce, his remark, addressed specifically to women (v. 11), seems to take for granted that some women are divorcing or are intending to do so. Whether women are contemplating divorce as a way to free themselves for spiritual pursuits or to free themselves from husbands whose spiritual pursuits preclude sexual relations is not certain. Paul's reminder to women that they should not attempt to remarry (to avoid adultery) seems to support the latter scenario.

Paul's next set of counsels concerns believers who are married to unbelievers. There is no reason for one who has become a believer to divorce an unbelieving spouse unless the unbeliever finds the believing partner's

is an unbeliever, and he is willing to go on living with her, she should not divorce her husband. [14]For the unbelieving husband is made holy through his wife, and the unbelieving wife is made holy through the brother. Otherwise your children would be unclean, whereas in fact they are holy.

[15]If the unbeliever separates, however, let him separate. The brother or sister is not bound in such cases; God has called you to peace. [16]For how do you know, wife, whether you will save your husband; or how do you know, husband, whether you will save your wife?

The Life That the Lord Has Assigned. [17]Only, everyone should live as the Lord has assigned, just as God called each one. I give this order in all the churches. [18]Was someone called after he had been circumcised? He should not try to undo his circumcision. Was an uncircumcised person called? He should not be circumcised. [19]Circumcision means nothing, and uncircumcision means nothing; what matters is keeping God's commandments. [20]Everyone should remain in the state in which he was called.

[21]Were you a slave when you were called? Do not be concerned but, even if you can gain your freedom, make the most of it. [22]For the slave called in the Lord is a freed person in the Lord, just as the free person who has been called is a slave of Christ. [23]You have been purchased at a price. Do not become

---

faith to be a problem and chooses to initiate the divorce. Then the believer is not bound. Otherwise, such marriages can be occasions of grace and holiness even for the non-believer and the couple's children.

7:17-24 Advice on one's social status

Although Paul may appear to digress in this subsection with the introduction of contrasting religious/ethnic statuses (circumcised-uncircumcised/Jew-Gentile) and social statuses (slave-free), this shift in focus allows Paul to continue to address the Corinthian situation from another angle. Apparently, some at Corinth are operating with the conviction that to really pursue the spiritual concerns proper to one's new Christian identity, one needs to change one's life circumstances or status, as if there were only one right or true life context or status appropriate to an authentic Christian life. By underscoring the insignificance of ritual identity markers/ethnicity and social status as a gauge for one's faithful obedience to God, Paul is able to illustrate the general principle he announces both at the beginning and the end of this subsection. This principle challenges the Corinthian assumption by establishing the fact that one's particular life context or social status in no way jeopardizes one's Christian freedom or ability to lead an authentic Christian existence. Thus there is no need for married people or any others to divest themselves of their particular set of circumstances.

slaves to human beings. ²⁴Brothers, everyone should continue before God in the state in which he was called.

Advice to Virgins and Widows. ²⁵Now in regard to virgins I have no commandment from the Lord, but I give my opinion as one who by the Lord's mercy is trustworthy. ²⁶So this is what I think best because of the present distress: that it is a good thing for a person to remain as he is. ²⁷Are you bound to a wife? Do not seek a separation. Are you free of a wife? Then do not look for a wife. ²⁸If you marry, however, you do not sin, nor does an unmarried woman sin if she marries; but such people will experience affliction in their earthly life, and I would like to spare you that.

²⁹I tell you, brothers, the time is running out. From now on, let those having wives act as not having them, ³⁰those weeping as not weeping, those rejoicing as not rejoicing, those buying as not owning, ³¹those using the world as not using it fully. For the world in its present form is passing away.

³²I should like you to be free of anxieties. An unmarried man is anxious about the things of the Lord, how he may please the Lord. ³³But a married man is anxious about the things of the world, how he may please his wife,

---

7:25-40 Advice to virgins/engaged couples, married women, and widows

In the remaining verses, Paul's advice is directed alternately to virgins/engaged couples (7:25-28 and 36-38), married women and widows (7:39-40), with a brief interlude (7:29-35) in which he offers an explanation for his consistent counsel to celibacy.

The question concerning virgins probably relates to whether an engaged but not yet married girl should proceed with marriage or remain unmarried. Paul advises celibacy but in the end leaves the decision up to the engaged couple, who do well whether they marry or not. Paul's insertion of the remark that the choice to marry is not a sin may have been necessitated by a contrary claim that marriage was sinful, an idea not unknown among early Christians (see 1 Tim 4:1-5). Paul's second reminder against divorce, now exclusively addressed to married women, may underscore the reality of wife-initiated divorce within the community. It is Paul's opinion that it is better for widowed women to remain unmarried.

Paul explains his preference for celibacy in view of the unfolding eschatological plan, an event of cosmic proportion. The world in its present form is passing away; human existence, with its characteristic forms, institutions, and priorities, is now relativized. Time is growing short, and the pressures will be intense in this brief interval before the unfolding begins. It is in light of this exigent situation that Paul counsels those who are unmarried to remain as they are, contrasting what he envisions as their total devotion to the Lord with the divided attention that characterizes the married. Indeed, Paul

51

³⁴and he is divided. An unmarried woman or a virgin is anxious about the things of the Lord, so that she may be holy in both body and spirit. A married woman, on the other hand, is anxious about the things of the world, how she may please her husband. ³⁵I am telling you this for your own benefit, not to impose a restraint upon you, but for the sake of propriety and adherence to the Lord without distraction.

³⁶If anyone thinks he is behaving improperly toward his virgin, and if a critical moment has come and so it has to be, let him do as he wishes. He is committing no sin; let them get married. ³⁷The one who stands firm in his resolve, however, who is not under compulsion but has power over his own will, and has made up his mind to keep his virgin, will be doing well. ³⁸So then, the one who marries his virgin does well; the one who does not marry her will do better.

³⁹A wife is bound to her husband as long as he lives. But if her husband dies, she is free to be married to whomever she wishes, provided that it be in the Lord. ⁴⁰She is more blessed, though, in my opinion, if she remains as she is, and I think that I too have the Spirit of God.

B. Offerings to Idols

8 **Knowledge Insufficient.** ¹Now in regard to meat sacrificed to idols: we realize that "all of us have knowledge"; knowledge inflates with pride, but love builds up. ²If anyone supposes he knows something, he does not yet know as he ought to know. ³But if one loves God, one is known by him.

⁴So about the eating of meat sacrificed to idols: we know that "there is no

---

prefers that all persons be free from the legitimate distractions of daily life in anticipation of the imminent coming of the Lord. Since Paul was not gifted with the charism of marriage, it is important to keep in mind that he speaks from the biased vantage point of a celibate. Clearly, stress, strain, and distraction are not the exclusive domain of the married. Thus we have to keep in mind that by Paul's best lights and in view of the eschatological exigency, he counsels celibacy as the better choice.

ARGUMENT CONCERNING FOOD OFFERED TO IDOLS

I Corinthians 8:1–11:1

In pagan cities such as Corinth, a good part of social life involved participation in cultic banquets at the temple, where meat sacrificed to idols was consumed, or at private dinner parties, where hosts served their guests sacrificed meat that went from the temple to local butcher shops, where it was purchased for consumption in private settings. Did the Corinthians, now converted from their former pagan ways, need to refrain from eating this meat? The community was divided in its response to this

idol in the world," and that "there is no God but one." [5]Indeed, even though there are so-called gods in heaven and on earth (there are, to be sure, many ◄ "gods" and many "lords"), [6]yet for us there is

> one God, the Father,
>> from whom all things are and
>>> for whom we exist,
>> and one Lord, Jesus Christ,
>>> through whom all things are and
>>>> through whom we exist.

Practical Rules. [7]But not all have this knowledge. There are some who have been so used to idolatry up until now that, when they eat meat sacrificed to idols, their conscience, which is weak, is defiled.

[8]Now food will not bring us closer to God. We are no worse off if we do not eat, nor are we better off if we do. [9]But make sure that this liberty of yours in no way becomes a stumbling block to the weak. [10]If someone sees you, with your ►

question, with its complicated theological and social implications, and apparently referred the issue to Paul, who responds from the angle of Christian knowledge and the exercise of rights and responsibility. In terms of literary composition, this unit is arranged according to the A (ch. 8) B (ch. 9) A' (ch. 10) pattern. In terms of rhetoric, there are four movements plus a summary which need to be considered.

8:1-13 Concern for others trumps knowledge as a criterion for action

Paul begins by citing another Corinthian slogan but notes that knowledge is not an unqualified good. It can puff up with pride, whereas love builds up. Paul even registers doubt that the enlightened ones' knowledge is as complete as they claim. Apparently some Corinthians, presumably those whom Paul had already chastised for their arrogance, argued in view of their superior knowledge that there was no reason to forego eating meat sacrificed to idols. An idol had no existence; therefore, so-called idol meat was just meat.

Judging from Paul's remark at verse 10 about reclining at table in the temple, it appears that the enlightened were arguing in view of their knowledge that they could continue to participate in the cultic banquets at the temple. However, "the weak" (in context, the less intellectually sophisticated) understood such eating to be charged with religious significance. They were apparently shocked that others would continue this practice. Perhaps they were even shocked at the continued social intermingling with pagans that this practice would presumably entail.

In principle, Paul agrees with the intellectuals. They are operating with sound theological principles. Idols do not exist. There is only one God. Objectively speaking, Paul could even agree that a decision to continue

knowledge, reclining at table in the temple of an idol, may not his conscience too, weak as it is, be "built up" to eat the meat sacrificed to idols? ¹¹Thus through your knowledge, the weak person is brought to destruction, the brother for whom Christ died. ¹²When you sin in this way against your brothers and wound their consciences, weak as they are, you are sinning against Christ. ¹³Therefore, if food causes my brother to sin, I will never eat meat again, so that I may not cause my brother to sin.

9 **Paul's Rights as an Apostle.** ¹Am I not free? Am I not an apostle? Have I not seen Jesus our Lord? Are you not my work in the Lord? ²Although I may not be an apostle for others, certainly I am for you, for you are the seal of my apostleship in the Lord.

³My defense against those who would pass judgment on me is this. ⁴Do we not have the right to eat and drink? ⁵Do we not have the right to take along a Christian wife, as do the rest of the apostles, and the brothers of the Lord,

---

eating idol meat followed logically from what they and he knew to be true. Thus Paul is not questioning the legitimacy of their right in regard to idol meat. However, he makes it clear that knowledge, even when rooted in sound theological principle, is not the exclusive criterion for determining praxis. Concern for other members of the community must take precedence over the exercise of a legitimate individual right.

Earlier Paul reminded the enlightened that their exercise of freedom was circumscribed by their belonging to God in Christ (6:19). Here he explicitly adds the other dimension that circumscribes the Christian exercise of freedom—the community. To scandalize any member of the community by the arrogant and complacent exercise of a right, which in the case of eating idol meat brings no benefit to anyone (v. 9) and scandal to some, simply because it can be justified in principle, amounts to a sin against the weaker brother, indeed against Christ. The phrase "against Christ" refers to the whole communion of believers, who together are later identified as the body of Christ (12:12). Thus Paul firmly warns against exercising rights, no matter how legitimate, to the detriment of one member, which is to say, to the detriment of all. He concludes this subunit of argumentation in the first person, injecting the course of action he would follow, which clearly depends on renouncing one's right out of love and concern for the entire community.

9:1-27 Renunciation of rights: an illustration based on Paul's praxis

Chapter 9 appears to be a departure from Paul's discussion of the right to eat idol meat. A closer look at this subunit reveals that it is an integral part of his argument. Here Paul problematizes his apostolic freedom in order to stress his renunciation of this freedom and thus provide a model of Christian praxis for the community. With regard to the right to eat idol

and Cephas? ⁶Or is it only myself and Barnabas who do not have the right not to work? ⁷Who ever serves as a soldier at his own expense? Who plants a vineyard without eating its produce? Or who shepherds a flock without using some of the milk from the flock? ⁸Am I saying this on human authority, or does not the law also speak of these things? ⁹It is written in the law of Moses, "You shall not muzzle an ox while it is treading out the grain." Is God concerned about oxen, ¹⁰or is he not really speaking for our sake? It was written for our sake, because the plowman should plow in hope, and the thresher in hope of receiving a share. ¹¹If we have sown spiritual seed for you, is it a great thing that we reap a material harvest from you? ¹²If others share this rightful claim on you, do not we still more?

---

meat, Paul has just argued that Christians must consider not only their freedom to exercise this right but also the possibility of freely renouncing that right when it negatively impacts others in the community. Indeed, this is what Paul said he would do (8:13).

Now, in chapter 9, Paul provides a model of renunciation in view of his own apostolic lifestyle and practice. He begins by building a strong case for his apostolic right to financial support. He is free. He is an apostle, and he has all the rights of every other apostle.

Paul first establishes these rights by reference to apostolic practice in verses 4-6, followed by simple examples based on the soldier, the vine planter, and the shepherd in verse 7. All these are supported by their trade. Paul supplements his argument by reference to a Mosaic law that prescribes recompense in the form of food even for oxen (vv. 8-9)! In verses 10-11, Paul further establishes his rights in view of the extent and the quality of his relationship with the Corinthians. Paul has shared spiritual blessing with them and is entitled to material recompense, even more so than other ministers.

After interjecting that he has renounced all these rights for the sake of the gospel (v. 12), Paul resumes the case for his own rights in view of a tradition associated with both Jewish and pagan practice, namely, the recompense of temple personnel who carried out the sacrifices at the altar. They were entitled to a portion of the sacrifice.

The final argument Paul calls upon to establish his right to support is the command of the Lord (see Luke 10:7) concerning recompense for the preachers of the gospel.

With his rights firmly established, Paul again affirms that he has freely given up the exercise of these rights (v. 15) and makes it clear that his purpose in writing about this is not to oblige the community to recompense

Reason for Not Using His Rights. Yet we have not used this right. On the contrary, we endure everything so as not to place an obstacle to the gospel of Christ. ¹³Do you not know that those who perform the temple services eat [what] belongs to the temple, and those who minister at the altar share in the sacrificial offerings? ¹⁴In the same way, the Lord ordered that those who preach the gospel should live by the gospel.

¹⁵I have not used any of these rights, however, nor do I write this that it be done so in my case. I would rather die. Certainly no one is going to nullify my boast. ¹⁶If I preach the gospel, this is no reason for me to boast, for an obligation has been imposed on me, and woe to me if I do not preach it! ¹⁷If I do so willingly, I have a recompense, but if unwillingly, then I have been entrusted with a stewardship. ¹⁸What then is my recompense?

---

him. He then proceeds in a roundabout way to explain his motives for setting aside his rights. In effect, he says that he did not undertake the work of preaching the gospel of his own volition; instead, it was an obligation imposed on him by God. Paul will do this, whether willingly or unwillingly, because he is compelled by God. Thus there is no cause for boasting in this. But he is quite proud of the fact that he has not taken advantage of the right to support that comes with this commission. On the contrary, he says that the only recompense he desires is no recompense at all! In offering the gospel free of charge, Paul renounces his right to support and presents himself as an exemplar of renunciation of rights.

Paul's argument becomes clearer in verses 19-23. In a series of rhetorical statements, he describes his missionary strategy of adaptability in order to accomplish his goal of winning as many as possible to the gospel. He presents himself as willingly living by the cultural, ethnic, and intellectual constraints of others in the service of the gospel; hence his reference to having become a "slave." To the intellectually sophisticated at Corinth, for whom freedom and the exercise of rights go hand in hand, the idea of renouncing one's rights can only appear to be weakness and foolishness. But Paul's slavish freedom is, paradoxically, true freedom manifested in the ability to adapt one's self to the needs of others. While the intellectuals at Corinth exercise their rights to the scandal and destruction of the weak, Paul's renunciation of rights, a true act of freedom, is ordered to the opposite end, namely, to save.

After using his own apostolic lifestyle as a model of freedom for the renunciation of rights, Paul now concludes this subunit of argumentation by exhorting the community to a life of discipline and self-control that supersedes the immediate concern of idol meat and its renunciation (vv. 24-27). The sports imagery employed by Paul makes perfect sense to anyone aware

That, when I preach, I offer the gospel free of charge so as not to make full use of my right in the gospel.

All Things to All. ¹⁹Although I am free in regard to all, I have made myself a slave to all so as to win over as many as possible. ²⁰To the Jews I became like a Jew to win over Jews; to those under the law I became like one under the law—though I myself am not under the law—to win over those under the law. ²¹To those outside the law I became like one outside the law—though I am not outside God's law but within the law of Christ—to win over those outside the law. ²²To the weak I became weak, to win over the weak. I have become all things to all, to save at least some. ²³All this I do for the sake of the gospel, so that I too may have a share in it.

²⁴Do you not know that the runners in the stadium all run in the race, but only one wins the prize? Run so as to win. ²⁵Every athlete exercises discipline in every way. They do it to win a perishable crown, but we an imperishable one. ²⁶Thus I do not run aimlessly; I do not fight as if I were shadowboxing. ²⁷No, I drive my body and train it, for fear that, after having preached to others, I myself should be disqualified.

10 **Warning against Overconfidence.** ¹I do not want you to be unaware, brothers, that our ancestors were all under the cloud and all passed through the sea, ²and all of them were baptized into Moses in the cloud and in the sea. ³All ate the same spiritual food, ⁴and all drank the same spiritual drink, for they drank from a spiritual rock that followed them, and the rock was the Christ. ⁵Yet God was not pleased with most of them, for they were struck down in the desert.

---

of the rigors of an athlete's life and would not be lost on the competitive Corinthians, whose city was home to the famous Isthmian games. Calling to mind the extent to which athletes train and discipline themselves in order to win a crown woven of perishable leaves, Paul exhorts the Corinthians to exercise and discipline themselves all the more, since they aspire to an imperishable crown. The Corinthians cannot be complacent as if they were running without a purpose or simply punching at air; rather, they must train and drive themselves to win this crown. In context, the self-discipline that Paul exhorts is aimed, above all, at the Corinthian intellectuals. Rather than complacently exercising their rights to the detriment of others, they need to practice restraint for the sake of the whole community.

10:1-13 Complacency and God's wrath: an example based on Israel's past
Paul's account of his own apostolic practice was intended as an exemplary lesson on the exercise of Christian freedom and served to develop and illustrate the point made in 8:13. Now Paul directs his attention to the complacent attitude of the Corinthian intellectuals, whose self-satisfaction with their own knowledge and exercise of rights is bringing them to flirt

◄ ⁶These things happened as examples for us, so that we might not desire evil things, as they did. ⁷And do not become idolaters, as some of them did, as it is written, "The people sat down to eat and drink, and rose up to revel." ⁸Let us not indulge in immorality as some of them did, and twenty-three ◄ thousand fell within a single day. ⁹Let us not test Christ as some of them did, and suffered death by serpents. ¹⁰Do not grumble as some of them did, and suffered death by the destroyer. ¹¹These ► things happened to them as an example, and they have been written down as a warning to us, upon whom the end of the ages has come. ¹²Therefore, whoever thinks he is standing secure should take care not to fall. ¹³No ► trial has come to you but what is

---

with idolatry. In addition to the problem of scandal, Paul is concerned that the Corinthian intellectuals are courting disaster by frequenting pagan temples, believing that they are beyond polytheistic superstitions and practices. Paul considers their actions a preamble to their own undoing. To illustrate and warn against such an outcome, he cites the example of Israel, whose complacency incurred the wrath of God.

In 1 Corinthians 10:1-4, Paul showcases the spiritual endowments of Israel. These verses contain allusions to select episodes from Israel's exodus (see Exod 13–14) and wilderness experience (see Exod 16–17; Num 20–21). Paul retells the stories, stressing the fact that all the Israelites enjoyed God's deliverance and protection, and all were sustained on the wilderness journey by God's providence. In his retelling of these episodes, Paul uses language that is clearly anachronistic, referring to Israel's exodus as a "baptism," specifically a baptism into Moses (v. 2), and their nourishment as a type of unifying spiritual communion underscored by the repetition of "all" and "the same" (v. 3). Paul even metaphorically identifies Christ with the water-giving rock which, according to Jewish legend, followed Israel in the desert.

Paul's point here is not to suggest that the Israelites had Christian sacraments; rather, he is attempting to create an analogy between the experience of Israel and that of the Corinthians. Though seemingly complicated in its presentation, the point is simple. As one people, Israel experienced powerful spiritual signs of God's favor and all the spiritual nourishment necessary to sustain them. Yet, despite such spiritual endowments, they still incurred God's wrath and were destroyed (v. 5). Israel took God's gifts for granted as signs of immunity from God's wrath and continued in idolatrous and immoral ways.

In a series of examples underscoring Israel's self-destructive behavior (vv. 6-10), Paul warns the Corinthians to avoid this kind of presumptuous

human. God is faithful and will not let you be tried beyond your strength; but with the trial he will also provide a way out, so that you may be able to bear it.

Warning against Idolatry. [14]Therefore, my beloved, avoid idolatry. [15]I am speaking as to sensible people; judge for yourselves what I am saying. [16]The cup of blessing that we bless, is it not a participation in the blood of Christ? The bread that we break, is it not a participation in the body of Christ? [17]Because the

---

conduct. The reference to Israel's sitting down to eat and drink (v. 7) recalls the erection of an altar of sacrifice to the golden calf (Exod 32) and Israel's subsequent feasting and rising up to revel (i.e., worship) this idol. This is a particularly apt reference for the Corinthians, who think they are secure in their knowledge and immune from idolatry. However, by going off to apparently innocuous feasting with their pagan friends in the venues associated with their former pagan lives, they are not above becoming entangled in idol worship. Moreover, as no amount of spiritual security saved the Israelites, who persisted in sexual immorality (v. 8), so likewise, if the Corinthians persist in sexual immorality, neither will they be saved. In case the self-styled intellectuals at Corinth could possibly miss the point of this story-telling, Paul makes it clear: If you think you stand secure in your knowledge, watch out! Others who believed themselves just as secure fell (v. 12).

Though Paul's concluding words of reassurance appear to, they do not negate the stern warning. On the contrary, the reassurance makes the warning all the more urgent. God is faithful and will assist the Corinthians with the testing and trials that they are bound to encounter. However, when through their arrogant reliance on their own power and knowledge rather than on God's power and wisdom they bring upon themselves testing and trials, then they are certain to fall as Israel did! Hence, rather than boasting in the exercise of this right to eat idol meat, which is intended to showcase their superior knowledge and unconstrained freedom, they ought to shun the practice.

10:14-22 Against communion with idols: judge for yourselves

As chapter 9 looked back to the discussion of chapter 8 and served to illumine and illustrate the need for renunciation of rights, 1 Corinthians 10:1-13, with its warning rooted in the example of Israel, looks forward to 1 Corinthians 10:14-22, where Paul now argues against participation at temple banquets. After the command to flee idolatry, Paul appeals to the Corinthians as "sensible people," a phrase that may be laced with sarcasm. Whatever the case, in view of the analogical argument he is about to

loaf of bread is one, we, though many, are one body, for we all partake of the one loaf.

¹⁸Look at Israel according to the flesh; are not those who eat the sacrifices participants in the altar? ¹⁹So what am I saying? That meat sacrificed to idols is anything? Or that an idol is anything? ²⁰No, I mean that what they sacrifice, [they sacrifice] to demons, not to God, and I do not want you to become participants with demons. ²¹You cannot drink the cup of the Lord and also the cup of demons. You cannot partake of the table of the Lord and of the table of demons. ²²Or are we provoking the Lord to jealous anger? Are we stronger than he?

---

set forth, Paul expects them to judge for themselves whether frequenting temple banquets is an innocuous practice.

Paul begins with what he and the Corinthians would agree on: participation in the Lord's Supper is an actual sharing in the blood and body of Christ, which effects a solidarity or bonding among believers and with Christ. The emphasis here is on the "sharing" and the oneness or solidarity effected (v. 18). Thus one cannot participate and intend non-solidarity, since the very act of participation produces it. It is clear that Paul does not recognize any dichotomy between the act of participation and the participant's intention.

As a second example of the bonding and solidarity effected through meal participation, Paul cites the historical example of the Jews ("Israel according to the flesh," v. 18). Their participation in the "altar" is Paul's way of saying they joined themselves to God. Both examples illustrate that eating a meal in the presence of God effects a solidarity between the community and God whom it worships.

Now Paul can go forward to draw a conclusion based on analogy: if eating a meal sacrificed to God effects solidarity with God, then eating a meal sacrificed to idols effects communion with idols. But Paul cannot draw this conclusion without contradicting what he had said previously (8:1-6). Aware of this (v. 19), he restates the conviction that an idol is nothing, and moves the analogy forward by substituting the term "demons" (v. 20). In referring to demons, Paul probably has in mind Deuteronomy 32:16-17. Based on this text, a Jewish tradition evolved which, while discounting the existence and divinity of anyone or thing but God alone, acknowledged the existence of demonic powers, variously referred to as gods or "idols," that actively opposed the purposes of God in the world. Apparently picking up on this tradition, Paul denies the existence of actual pagan idols but acknowledges the existence of supernatural powers. Since the absolute exclusiveness of the solidarity with God in Christ pre-

Seek the Good of Others. ²³"Everything is lawful," but not everything is beneficial. "Everything is lawful," but not everything builds up. ²⁴No one should seek his own advantage, but that of his neighbor. ²⁵Eat anything sold in the market, without raising questions on grounds of conscience, ²⁶for "the earth and its fullness are the Lord's." ²⁷If an unbeliever invites you and you want to go, eat whatever is placed before you, without raising questions on grounds of conscience. ²⁸But if someone says to you, "This was offered in sacrifice," do not eat it on account of the one who called attention to it and on account of conscience; ²⁹I mean not your own conscience, but the other's. For why should my freedom be determined by someone else's conscience? ³⁰If I partake thankfully, why am I reviled for that over which I give thanks?

³¹So whether you eat or drink, or whatever you do, do everything for the glory of God. ³²Avoid giving offense, whether to Jews or Greeks or the church of God, ³³just as I try to please everyone in every way, not seeking my own benefit but that of the many, that they may be saved.

---

cludes any other union, the enlightened ones have to make a choice: participation at the table of demons or the table of the Lord. The Corinthians cannot have it both ways.

Paul concludes this section with two rhetorical questions. The first reverts back to the example of Israel set out in 10:1-13 and recalls the destruction that accompanied their complacency. Lest any of the enlightened ones doubt a similar outcome if they continue at cultic banquets, Paul leaves them with a final question that puts their presumed knowledge and power in perspective. Perhaps they are intellectually stronger than the weak. But are they stronger than the Lord? The answer is clear.

10:23–11:1 Summary: seek the good of others

In his argument so far, Paul gives a single response, in light of two separate criteria, to the question of participation in temple banquets. First, the practice should be renounced out of love and concern for the other members of the community (8:1-13 argument plus 9:1-27 example). Second, the practice should be renounced because participants in temple banquets implicate themselves in idolatrous worship and risk incurring God's wrath (10:1-13 example plus 10:14-22 argument).

Now, in the final subsection of this extended argument concerning food offered to idols, Paul considers whether meat sacrificed to idols can be consumed in non-cultic, private settings. Paul's discussion is framed by two concerns: that freedom is exercised in view of what is upbuilding for the community (v. 24) and that whatever activity is undertaken should be directed to the glory of God (v. 31). Within this framework, Paul con-

11
¹Be imitators of me, as I am of Christ.

IV. Problems in Liturgical Assemblies

²I praise you because you remember me in everything and hold fast to the traditions, just as I handed them on to you.

A. Women's Headresses

Man and Woman. ³But I want you to know that Christ is the head of every man, and a husband the head of his wife, and God the head of Christ. ⁴Any man who prays or prophesies with his head covered brings shame upon his head. ⁵But any woman who prays or

---

siders the eating of previously sacrificed meat purchased at the market and eaten in a believer's own home or at a dinner party in the home of an unbeliever to be a legitimate practice, which, of itself, does not contravene either of the two concerns. Presumably, the enlightened at Corinth already know this. It is the weak who need to understand that eating sacrificed meat in private venues is a legitimate exercise of freedom. Thus informed, the weak need to overcome their scruples and cease to create problems where they do not exist.

In verses 28-29 Paul adds a proviso enjoining renunciation if "someone" in any private setting calls attention to the meat's origin. Paul does not identify the informer as a believer. Regardless, this proviso is part of the ethic of concern for others that Paul is attempting to instill in the community. Modeled on Christ's example of selfless love, Christian freedom seeks the good of others and the glory of God. It is neither constrained by unwarranted scrupulosity nor simply ordered to self-satisfaction. As one whose praxis is rooted in imitation of Jesus, who sought the salvation of many, Paul's call to the Corinthians to imitate him is ultimately a call to live Christlike lives.

ARGUMENTS CONCERNING ASPECTS OF COMMUNITY WORSHIP
1 Corinthians 11:2–14:40

In this next major section of 1 Corinthians, Paul sets out three separate arguments that are linked by the fact that each concerns problematic behavior affecting the community's worship. Without mentioning the source of his information, he first deals with a problem relating to the hairstyles of some community members praying and prophesying at the liturgical assembly (11:2-16). A more serious problem, which Paul has learned of through oral sources, concerns abuses and divisions at the Eucharist, the very sign and source of the community's unity, which is being negated by their behavior (11:17-34). Finally, in a lengthy argument con-

prophesies with her head unveiled brings shame upon her head, for it is one and the same thing as if she had had her head shaved. ⁶For if a woman does not have her head veiled, she may as well have her hair cut off. But if it is shameful for a woman to have her hair cut off or her head shaved, then she should wear a veil.

⁷A man, on the other hand, should not cover his head, because he is the image and glory of God, but woman is the glory of man. ⁸For man did not come from woman, but woman from man; ⁹nor was man created for woman, but woman for man; ¹⁰for this reason a woman should have a sign of authority on her head, because of the angels.

cerning spiritual gifts (12:1-14:40), a topic presumably raised by the Corinthians in their letter, Paul deals with the problems created by the misguided desire of some to show their superior spiritual status by flaunting certain spiritual gifts and deprecating others.

Argument concerning hairstyles (11:2-16)

11:2-16 Liturgy and hair etiquette

The logical sequel to Paul's remark at 11:2, concerning traditions, seems to be the discussion at 11:17-34. Though the community is faithful to the traditions, which earns Paul's praise (11:2), their behavior at the Eucharist, not their hairdos, is an exception to this fidelity to tradition, which earns Paul's censure (11:17). Thus 11:3-16 appears to be out of place in its current literary context. Not surprisingly, some commentators argue that verses 3-16 were a later insertion into the text. However, this need not be the case. If the Corinthians had raised this issue, Paul may have felt compelled to give a response, which, however awkwardly, he locates here along with other responses about issues affecting community worship. In addition to the awkward fit, the exact nature of the problem is somewhat obscure, as is Paul's argumentation.

What can be inferred from 11:3-16 is that in the context of the liturgical assembly some women *and* men, as is clear from 11:4, were transgressing codes relating to hair etiquette, which apparently upset others in the community. Contrary to custom, some women were praying and prophesying with their hair unbound, while some men, likewise engaged, wore their hair long. The mention of having one's hair cut off (vv. 6-7) and the later references to long hair (vv. 15-17) suggest that hairstyles, not head coverings or veils, are under discussion. Why some in the community felt free to abandon this custom is a matter of speculation. Some hypothesize that the transgressors were attempting to concretely express the extinction of

¹¹Woman is not independent of man or man of woman in the Lord. ¹²For just as woman came from man, so man is born of woman; but all things are from God.

¹³Judge for yourselves: is it proper for a woman to pray to God with her head unveiled? ¹⁴Does not nature itself teach you that if a man wears his hair

---

ethnic, status, and gender distinctions presumed to be the intent of Paul's baptism/new creation preaching (see, e.g., Gal 3:27-28; 2 Cor 5:16-17). Regardless of their motivation, Paul rejects the abandonment of the custom relating to hairstyles.

To make his case, Paul begins his argument by establishing a schema of relationships (vv. 3-4). Obviously, Paul does not intend the word "head" in the literal sense. As a metaphor, it is most often understood to stand for "authority over" or "source of," although other renderings are possible. Whatever the case, in Paul's schematic formulation, the point is that one member of the pair is precedent and preeminent with regard to the other. Within this logic Paul insists that how one acts either honors or dishonors one's figurative head/source. Men who transgress the hair etiquette dishonor Christ, while women dishonor the men of the community (vv. 4-6).

Paul does not explain why a particular hairstyle is an occasion of dishonor to one's figurative head/source. However, it requires no stretch of the imagination to get the connection. Even in our own day, clothing, hairstyles, tattoos, body piercing, and the like are often construed as positive or negative reflectors of parents, schools, or other institutions thought to have some investment in the person under scrutiny. In the Mediterranean culture of Paul's day, unbound hair on a woman was associated with sexual permissiveness, and short-cropped hair was associated with lesbianism and prostitution, while men with long hair were thought to be effeminate.

With regard to the presence of a woman with unbound hair at the assembly, Paul would be objecting to her appearance as a sexually loose or available woman. In reference to men praying and prophesying with long hair and women with cropped hair, if the latter was an actual case (which is not clear from the text), Paul would be objecting to the blurring of gender distinctions caused by the adoption of inappropriate hairstyles.

A second argument is unfolded in verses 7-12. The contrast stated in verse 7 is explicated in verses 8-9, where, in reference to the account of creation in Genesis 2, Paul explains his claim that woman is the reflected glory of man in view of her having been made from him. Consequently, a woman is expected to avoid anything that dishonors a man. Thus she must keep her hair bound.

long it is a disgrace to him, [15]whereas if a woman has long hair it is her glory, because long hair has been given [her] for a covering? [16]But if anyone is inclined to be argumentative, we do not have such a custom, nor do the churches of God.

B. The Lord's Supper

An Abuse at Corinth. [17]In giving this instruction, I do not praise the fact that your meetings are doing more harm than good. [18]First of all, I hear that ▶ when you meet as a church there are divisions among you, and to a degree I believe it; [19]there have to be factions among you in order that [also] those who are approved among you may become known. [20]When you meet in one ▶ place, then, it is not to eat the Lord's supper, [21]for in eating, each one goes

What Paul intends in verse 10 is an enigma. It is not certain whether he is expressing an additional claim that a woman needs her hair bound because of "the angels" or whether verse 10 is an implication deriving from verses 8-9. Paul could be alluding to the belief that angels, considered the protectors of the order of creation, were present as the custodians of the liturgy. The enigmatic expression "have authority over her head" may mean that the woman should take charge of her own head and keep her hair bound in view of the order and decorum of the liturgy, over which the angels stood guard.

Paul's statements stressing the reciprocity between man and woman (vv. 11-12) need not be taken as a contradiction of what he has previously argued; rather, Paul makes two equally valid observations. Men and women are equal and interdependent. As such, they have an equal right to pray and prophesy in the church, and hence to assume roles of liturgical leadership. This equality, however, does not allow for the abandonment of social norms or for the abolition of gender differences, which Paul believes are to be maintained through external markers, namely, long, bound hair for women and short hair for men. Paul's assertion of the equality and interdependence of men and women, notwithstanding gender difference, is usually overlooked by those who view this entire passage as a statement of the absolute subordination of women.

In the concluding verses, Paul adds a third and fourth argument, neither of which is developed. The third argument appeals to what nature teaches, by which Paul must mean that long hair is inappropriate for men and appropriate for women (vv. 14-15). The fourth and final argument appeals to the custom of the churches of God (v. 16). In case the Corinthians are not persuaded by his three preceding arguments, Paul adds this last appeal to remind the Corinthians that, in any case, they ought to conform their practice to that of all believers.

ahead with his own supper, and one goes hungry while another gets drunk. ²²Do you not have houses in which you can eat and drink? Or do you show con- tempt for the church of God and make those who have nothing feel ashamed? What can I say to you? Shall I praise you? In this matter I do not praise you.

Argument concerning division and abuses at the Lord's Supper (11:17-34)

11:17-22 Your meetings do more harm than good

Paul's commendation of the Corinthians at 11:2 was perhaps part of his rhetorical strategy to prepare the community for the rebuke with which he begins his discussion of their behavior at the Eucharist (v. 17). Paul's next statement, namely, that he has heard about divisions within the community (v. 18)—as if he were unaware of such divisions—has led many to conclude that 1 Corinthians must be a composite of at least two letters. However, the additional remark "and to a degree I believe it" is a bit of mocking sarcasm. Paul knows well the extent of the divisiveness in the community. Since it has invaded even their Eucharist assembly, Paul now observes that more harm than good results from this coming to- gether. Verse 19 should probably be taken as a continuation of Paul's mocking. What else can be expected but divisions when some community members are still concerned only about their own individual status, well- being, and self-satisfaction!

To understand Paul's comments, it is helpful to recall that in earliest Christianity the Lord's Supper was not the highly ritualized, one-hour event in a church to which we are accustomed. Smaller assemblies of be- lievers at Corinth would gather at the home of the head of one such as- sembly, whose house would have been large enough to accommodate the entire community. There all believers gathered as one to eat an actual meal, during which they shared the bread and cup of the Lord's Supper, the sign and source of their unity. But Paul says even though they are as- sembled for this purpose, each comes to eat "his own supper," not to eat the "Lord's supper" (v. 20), with the result that some are sated while oth- ers go without and are even made to feel ashamed (v. 22).

Sometimes Paul's rhetoric is taken as a description of the economic disparity within the community that is thought to underlie the problem discussed here. However, economic disparity is only one aspect of a much larger picture. Established social convention dictated that rank and status be acknowledged by one's place at table and the amount and quality of food and drink one was apportioned. When this larger picture is consid-

Tradition of the Institution. ²³For I received from the Lord what I also handed on to you, that the Lord Jesus, on the night he was handed over, took bread, ²⁴and, after he had given thanks, broke it and said, "This is my body that is for you. Do this in remembrance of me." ²⁵In the same way also the cup, after supper, saying, "This cup is the new covenant in my blood. Do this, as often as you drink it, in remembrance of me." ²⁶For as often as you eat this bread and drink the cup, you proclaim the death of the Lord until he comes.

²⁷Therefore whoever eats the bread or drinks the cup of the Lord unworthily will have to answer for the body and blood of the Lord. ²⁸A person should examine himself, and so eat the bread and drink the cup. ²⁹For anyone

---

ered, it appears that Paul's overriding concern is that societal norms are being used as the standard of comportment at the Eucharist. These norms encourage divisions and self-aggrandizement and promote self-serving behavior, all of which undermine the unity of the community and negate the whole purpose of the Eucharist. If members' only purpose in coming is to serve their own needs and eat to their own satisfaction, then they ought to stay in their own homes (v. 22). Whatever the Corinthians think of themselves, Paul makes it clear that he cannot praise them.

11:23-26 The tradition of the institution

To call the Corinthians back to their senses, Paul reminds them of the tradition concerning the founding of this communal meal (vv. 23-26). Since Paul's letter antedates Mark, the first Gospel, by almost fifteen years, we have here the earliest preserved account of the institution of the Eucharist. Paul employs the technical terms "received" and "handed on" used in Jewish culture for the transmission of important traditions. This tradition is "from the Lord," meaning that the origin of this tradition of sharing the cup and bread is with the Lord himself. The community gathers in the *present* to observe *the Lord's* last supper, to recall the *past* historical event of Jesus' betrayal and self-sacrificing love symbolized in the bread and cup, and to proclaim this death until his *future* coming.

For Paul, the whole point of this coming together is to remember (vv. 25-26) the death of Christ and to allow the reality and meaning of that death to take form in their own lives. What matters to Paul is not the words of the tradition per se, but that the Corinthians live as one saved community rooted in the self-sacrificing love of Christ! Their self-serving behavior betrays Christ's self-sacrificing love and destroys the reality effected through his death. As such, they are not eating the "Lord's supper" (v. 20) but continuing in their own community-destroying ways.

who eats and drinks without discerning the body, eats and drinks judgment on himself. ³⁰That is why many among you are ill and infirm, and a considerable number are dying. ³¹If we discerned ourselves, we would not be under judgment; ³²but since we are judged by [the] Lord, we are being disciplined so that we may not be condemned along with the world.

³³Therefore, my brothers, when you come together to eat, wait for one another. ³⁴If anyone is hungry, he should eat at home, so that your meetings may not result in judgment. The other matters I shall set in order when I come.

11:27-32 The tradition and the situation in the Corinthian community

Paul now applies the tradition to the specific situation of abuse and division at the Lord's Supper. In context, verses 27-28 refer neither to a person's moral condition nor to the discernment of the Real Presence. Rather, to eat unworthily means to behave in a way that promotes divisions that are antithetical to the whole purpose of the Eucharist. Unworthy participants are responsible for the body and blood of the Lord, in the sense that they are held responsible for offending the community of believers who are the body of Christ. To eat and drink without "discerning the body" refers to the self-serving behavior that disregards the well-being and unity of the whole body of believers. Such blatant disregard is an act of self-incrimination (v. 29) through which those who eat unworthily bring God's judgment on themselves.

Exactly what Paul means in verse 30 remains an enigma. It seems, however, that he takes the illness and death of some members of the community as a sign that God's judgment has already befallen the community. Apparently Paul expects this to be taken as a warning by the Corinthians to discontinue their abusive behavior in order to avoid future condemnation (v. 32).

11:33-34 Practical advice

Paul concludes his discussion with pragmatic instructions in which he prescribes the behavior appropriate to Christians gathered to celebrate the source and sign of their unity. Above all, each one's behavior is to be characterized by consideration for the other. Temporal waiting is obviously a first step in showing consideration. However, beyond mere waiting, Paul probably also has in mind a true openness to and receptivity of the other born of the selfless love and desire for unity that the Eucharist is meant to symbolize and engender. Paul's notice in verse 34 that he defers the treatment of other unspecified matters to a future visit underscores the importance of this discussion about behavior at the Eucharist.

C. Spiritual Gifts

12 **Unity and Variety.** ¹Now in regard to spiritual gifts, brothers, I do not want you to be unaware. ²You know how, when you were pagans, you were constantly attracted and led away to mute idols. ³Therefore, I tell you that nobody speaking by the spirit of God says, "Jesus be accursed." And no one can say, "Jesus is Lord," except by the holy Spirit.

⁴There are different kinds of spiritual gifts but the same Spirit; ⁵there are different forms of service but the same Lord; ⁶there are different workings but the same God who produces all of them

---

Argument concerning spiritual gifts (12:1–14:40)

The expression "Now in regard to" at 12:1 indicates that Paul is about to begin a new argument, which extends from 12:1 through 14:40. This is Paul's final and lengthiest argument relating to a matter affecting community worship. In this particular argument, concerned with "spiritual gifts" (Greek: *pneumatika*), Paul addresses a problematic situation involving the use and abuse of spiritual gifts (Greek: *charismata*). Though Paul does not say, it is likely that he became aware of this situation from the Corinthians' letter to him.

What can be inferred from the argument is that competitiveness in the community revolving around the possession and manifestation of spiritual gifts deemed to be more superior, especially the much-vaunted gift of tongues, was threatening the unity of the community (ch. 12) and creating disorder and chaos at the community's prayer assembly (ch. 14). In response, Paul unfolds an argument in three segments, forming an ABA' pattern. Section A (= 12:4-31a) contains a general discussion that stresses both the need for unity in diversity and diversity in unity, while the A' section (= 14:1-40) is more specifically focused on the advantage of prophecy over speaking in tongues and the order that must obtain within the prayer assembly. In the middle B section (= 12:31b—13:13), a rhetorical digression, Paul develops and discloses the key motive that must inform the exercise of spiritual gifts, namely, Christian charity.

The whole issue under discussion in chapters 12–14 presumes a situation in the community at Corinth in which extraordinary spiritual gifts and their manifestation were an everyday reality in the life of the community. It is important to remember when reading the argument here that Paul is grateful for and acknowledges the inherent goodness of each spiritual gift with which the community has been endowed, including the gift of speaking in tongues (see 1:5). Unfortunately, some viewed their gifts, especially speaking in tongues, as tokens of superior spiritual status, exercised for

◀ in everyone. ⁷To each individual the manifestation of the Spirit is given for some benefit. ⁸To one is given through the Spirit the expression of wisdom; to another the expression of knowledge according to the same Spirit; ⁹to another ▶

---

self-aggrandizement. It is this skewed view and abusive use of the gifts that Paul rejects and seeks to correct by his discussion of the relative significance of each gift, whose exercise must be ordered to the upbuilding and unity of the whole community.

A variety of gifts from the same Spirit for the common good (12:1-31a)

In this first subunit of argumentation, Paul introduces the new topic (vv. 1-3) and then locates the origin of all spiritual gifts in the same divine source (vv. 4-11). A body analogy, commonly used in Greco-Roman speech to illustrate the relationship of the one and the many, is employed by Paul in verses 12-26 to stress the diversity and interdependence of community members. In conclusion, Paul applies this analogy directly to the situation at Corinth and ranks members in view of gifts and roles (vv. 27-31a).

12:1-3 Introduction

Paul's desire that the Corinthians not "be unaware" implies a certain ignorance about spiritual realities, despite the fact that some in the community are apparently posing as authorities on the subject, believing that the mere manifestation of certain spiritual gifts, especially ecstatic utterances, somehow makes them authentic spiritual persons. Paul corrects this assumption in the next two verses. In their former lives as pagans, the Corinthians may have been caught up in the thrill of ecstasy, but it was all futile, since they were swept off to dumb idols (v. 2). Thus their own experience underscores the fact that ecstatic experience and accompanying utterances, of themselves, cannot be the measure of what it means to be an authentically spiritual person.

The true test of whether one is guided by the Spirit of God is that one is able to confess that "Jesus is Lord" (v. 3). Paul contrasts this confession with the statement "Jesus be accursed." Rather than an actual utterance heard in the Corinthian prayer assembly, the latter statement should probably be taken as a rhetorical counterpoint introduced by Paul to dramatize the antithesis between what is authentically Spirit-empowered and what is not. For Paul, the acknowledgment of the Lordship of Jesus alone is the criterion by which one judges who lives in the realm of the Spirit and is authentically Spirit-inspired.

71

Statue of Caesar Augustus, the first Roman emperor

faith by the same Spirit; to another gifts of healing by the one Spirit; [10]to another mighty deeds; to another prophecy; to another discernment of spirits; to another varieties of tongues; to another interpretation of tongues. [11]But one and

---

12:4-11 Manifestations of the Spirit

Up until this point in his argument, Paul has spoken of spiritual realities *(pneumatika)*. Here in verse 4 he introduces the word "gifts" *(charismata)* for the first time. By redefining authentic spiritual realities as "gifts," Paul indirectly undermines Corinthian arrogance. No one has merited such gifts, and since each community member's gift derives from the same source, none is inherently inferior to another. Along with the diversity of gifts inspired by the Spirit, there are also various forms of service and workings that are also divinely ordained. All these gifts in all their diversity ultimately derive from God and are given through the agency of the Spirit. To each member of the community is given some manifestation of the Spirit (v. 7). Since the Spirit is manifest in the manifold gifts, services, and workings, any claim that any one particular gift, service, or working is a fuller manifestation of the Spirit is simply unwarranted. Moreover, to devalue any gift is to devalue the work of the Spirit. Thus, as arrogance is undermined by virtue of the fact that any manifestation of the Spirit is a gift, so also is the competitiveness that derives from the false assumption that certain manifestations are superior to others.

In the second half of verse 7, Paul now adds a second criterion for determining who is authentically spiritual and what is authentically Spirit-inspired. That which is an authentic manifestation of the Spirit must in some way benefit others. The manifestations are given neither for self-glorification nor for advancing one's own status but for the common good. When the latter is not the end toward which the public manifestation of the Spirit is ordered, it cannot be an authentic Spirit-inspired manifestation, nor can the person be authentically spiritual.

With these two criteria established, Paul proceeds to give a representative listing (compare with the list at 12:28 and Rom 12:6-8) of the manifestations of the Spirit in verses 8-11. In all, Paul mentions nine examples of the Spirit's manifestations in these three verses, portraying them as common occurrences in the community at Corinth. "Faith" (v. 9) is apparently a reference to a particular endowment for a special service (although Paul does not specify), and not the saving faith common to all believers.

Judging by Paul's discussion in chapter 14, it was the gift of tongues that was apparently creating most of the disturbance in the community.

the same Spirit produces all of these, distributing them individually to each person as he wishes.

One Body, Many Parts. ¹²As a body is one though it has many parts, and all the parts of the body, though many, are one body, so also Christ. ¹³For in one Spirit we were all baptized into one body, whether Jews or Greeks, slaves or free persons, and we were all given to drink of one Spirit.

¹⁴Now the body is not a single part, but many. ¹⁵If a foot should say, "Because I am not a hand I do not belong to the body," it does not for this reason belong any less to the body. ¹⁶Or if an ear should say, "Because I am not an eye I do not belong to the body," it does not for this reason belong any less to the body. ¹⁷If the whole body were an eye, where would the hearing be? If the whole body were hearing, where would

---

Paul's careful listing of these distinct yet all Spirit-inspired gifts at work in the community is probably intended to put this particular gift of tongues in its proper context. It is only one among many. The repetition of "to one/to another" and the "same/one Spirit" underscores both the activity of the Spirit, the source of each gift, and the importance of each individual member of the community whose gift, though different from that of another, contributes to and is necessary for the common good.

In verse 11, Paul concludes this subsection on gifts and succinctly restates the key points he has made so far: every distinct gift is the work of the Spirit. It is a gift freely given to individual believers through God's generous grace, to be exercised in the service of the church for the promotion of the common good.

12:12-26 Diversity in unity, unity in diversity

Paul now carries his points forward by means of an analogy between the church and the body. The body analogy was a common figure of speech in political discourse in antiquity. Human societies were compared to a body, whose well-being depended on each member of society knowing his or her place. Usually the analogy was employed to conserve the status quo, especially as a means to keep the lower classes in their place and dissuade them from dissent or rebellion that could upset the balance of power. Paul uses the analogy not to subordinate but to stress the diversity, interdependence, and importance of all the members of the community, who together form one body.

The analogy is introduced in 12:12, which concludes with the phrase "so also Christ," not with "so also the community/church" as one might expect. For Paul, the body of believers is Christ, or the body of Christ, a metaphoric expression he employs to express what he believes to be the

the sense of smell be? [18]But as it is, God placed the parts, each one of them, in the body as he intended. [19]If they were all one part, where would the body be? [20]But as it is, there are many parts, yet one body. [21]The eye cannot say to the hand, "I do not need you," nor again the head to the feet, "I do not need you." [22]Indeed, the parts of the body that seem to be weaker are all the more necessary, [23]and those parts of the body that we consider less honorable we surround with greater honor, and our less presentable parts are treated with greater propriety, [24]whereas our more presentable parts do not need this. But

---

reality of Christian existence. Believers are bound in a living unity with the risen Lord, which is effected through the unifying activity and presence of the Spirit in baptism (v. 13). Hence, though many, they form one body, the body of Christ.

Having established the analogy, Paul now stresses the need for diversity within this unity by means of an absurd staging of talking body parts announcing their liberation from the body (vv. 14-16)! The result of the withdrawal of any part, either in view of its superiority or inferiority to the other parts, would be a distorted entity, but not a body which, of its very nature, requires the diversity of parts (vv. 19-20). Paul's lesson is clear. A human body cannot be a body without the diversity of parts. Likewise, the body of Christ cannot be a body without each distinct believer, whose place and function in the body depend on God (v.18). Hence the diversity within the community is not a reality to be obliterated, nor even merely tolerated. It is essential.

Whereas in verses 14-20 Paul's stress is on the necessity of diversity in unity, in verses 21-26 the accent falls on the need to maintain unity amidst the diversity. No member of the community can afford to scorn any other member or set up divisive distinctions. The "weaker" and "less honorable" parts probably allude to community members who were looked down on either because of social status or lack of intellectual and spiritual sophistication or both. Paul reminds the arrogant of the community, who likely associate themselves with the more "presentable" or "honorable" parts, that those they scorn need to be honored and cared for. God has not differentiated among members as a basis for division, for there can be no division in the body, which relies on the interdependence of its parts for its functioning. Moreover, not only are the weakest links indispensable to the life of the community, but it is to these that God has given greater honor (v. 24). Thus if there is division and discord, the whole body suffers, because no member is independent of the other in the body of Christ.

God has so constructed the body as to give greater honor to a part that is without it, ²⁵so that there may be no division in the body, but that the parts may have the same concern for one another. ²⁶If [one] part suffers, all the parts suffer with it; if one part is honored, all the parts share its joy.

Application to Christ. ²⁷Now you are Christ's body, and individually parts of it. ²⁸Some people God has designated in the church to be, first, apostles; second, prophets; third, teachers; then, mighty deeds; then, gifts of healing, assistance, administration, and varieties of tongues. ²⁹Are all apostles? Are all prophets? Are all teachers? Do all work mighty deeds? ³⁰Do all have gifts of healing? Do all speak in tongues? Do all interpret? ³¹Strive eagerly for the greatest spiritual gifts.

The Way of Love. But I shall show you a still more excellent way.

12:27-30a Application to the church

The analogy is now directly applied to the community of believers, who are Christ's body. Within this body, God has gifted members with diverse gifts and functions. As with the preceding list (vv. 8-10), here, too, in verse 28, Paul seems to provide a representative rather than exhaustive list. He numerically ranks the first three. There is no way of knowing if the enumeration is intended to suggest a hierarchy of authority among these three. Minimally speaking, the enumeration suggests that Paul considered these three very important ministries.

The other gifts or functions, introduced by "then," parallel each other's importance, though they are probably of lesser importance than those enumerated. Once again Paul lists varieties of tongues last (see 12:10), apparently to reinforce the fact that tongues are only one among many gifts bestowed for the common good. Each of the concluding rhetorical questions begins with the Greek negative (*mē*), which always expects the answer no! No, all cannot have the same gift or perform the same function, and no one person can have all the gifts and perform all the functions. Here again Paul emphasizes the necessity for diversity in unity. Against the arrogant in Corinth, who apparently measure a member's spiritual endowment and worth in view of *one* gift, speaking in tongues, Paul asserts that diversity is not only good but necessary! Some of the Corinthians have unfortunately mistaken uniformity for unity. Paul wants the latter, which is only truly achieved when each member's distinct contribution is valued and incorporated with all others to build up the whole body.

◄ 13 ¹If I speak in human and angelic tongues but do not have love, I am a resounding gong or a clashing cymbal. ²And if I have the gift of prophecy and comprehend all mysteries and all knowledge; if I have all faith so as to move mountains but do not have love, I am nothing. ³If I give away everything I own, and if I hand my body over so that I may boast but do not have love, I gain nothing.

⁴Love is patient, love is kind. It is ► not jealous, [love] is not pompous, it is not inflated, ⁵it is not rude, it does not ► seek its own interests, it is not quick-tempered, it does not brood over injury, ⁶it does not rejoice over wrongdoing but rejoices with the truth. ⁷It bears all

---

Love, the more excellent way (13:1-13)

This poetic encomium (speech) in praise of love is often taken as an abstract meditation on love, with little connection to the discussion of spiritual gifts. However, in context this encomium is actually an integral part of Paul's argument in chapters 12–14, through which he presents love as the quality of Christian life par excellence and the absolute norm that must govern the exercise of the gifts of the Spirit. Verse 31 of chapter 12 introduces this poetic interlude, which begins at 13:1.

13:1-3 Gifts without love are of no account

Using himself as a hypothetical example, Paul asserts that without love the exercise of gifts is futile and empty. The first gift Paul mentions is tongues. Exercised apart from love, the tongues-speaker produces only a strident noise, like brass instruments struck without purpose. Though Paul begins with the Corinthians' prized gift, we must not hastily assume that his sole purpose here is to deflate the arrogant Corinthians by devaluing what is most important to them. This becomes apparent in verses 2-3, where Paul considers other gifts and practices. Even if one should prophesy, a gift Paul considers superior to tongues (see 14:5), or have extraordinary faith, without love this person is nothing. Likewise, should one choose a life of self-abnegation and hardship, as Paul himself did (see ch. 9), without love such practices are of no account. In sum, all gifts and religious practices are equally of no account unless motivated and informed by love.

13:4-7 In praise of love

Paul's praise of love personified begins with two positive statements in the first half of verse 4 and ends with one long verse extolling four of love's positive features (v. 7). From the second half of verse 4 through verse 6, Paul focuses on what love is not or does not do. In all, there are eight negative statements. Most of the negatives correspond directly or indirectly to

things, believes all things, hopes all things, endures all things.

◄ 8Love never fails. If there are prophecies, they will be brought to nothing; if tongues, they will cease; if knowledge, it will be brought to nothing. 9For we know partially and we prophesy partially, 10but when the perfect comes, the partial will pass away. 11When I was a child, I used to talk as a child, think as a child, reason as a child; when I became a man, I put aside childish things. 12At ► present we see indistinctly, as in a mirror, but then face to face. At present I

actual behavior of the Corinthians already criticized by Paul. For example, "jealous" and "inflated" (v. 4b) recall behavior and attitudes that Paul castigated in chapters 1–4 and 5. To "rejoice over wrongdoing" (v. 6) probably alludes to behavior censured in chapters 5 and 6. "Does not seek its own interest" (v. 5) evokes Paul's discussion of meat offered to idols and the renunciation of one's rights in the interest of others (chs. 8–10).

Thus Paul's list of negatives is not merely a poetic extolling of the abstract notion of love but a rather pointed indictment of the Corinthians' behavior. By all counts, Corinthian behavior is devoid of Christian love. In view of the assertions of verses 1-3, the Corinthians should realize that their exercise of gifts and other religious practices is entirely void. They have gained nothing by their displays. They are nothing, despite their own exalted self-perception.

In verse 7, Paul summarizes positively the character of love. Belief and hope are focused on the future. Strengthened by them, Christians are enabled to bear and endure in the present. Especially in view of the repeated "all things," Paul's statement in verse 7 can unfortunately be read as an exhortation to suffer any kind of abuse, believe anything, or maintain hope at all costs, even when unrealistic. Far from promoting abusive, self-destructive, or self-deceptive behavior, here Paul advocates behavior governed by love that transcends the self-interest, jealousy, and competitiveness leading to strife and division and promotes reconciliation and unity.

13:8-13 The abiding nature of love

Paul now advances his argument for the preeminence of love in view of its enduring character in contrast to gifts, all of which are temporal. Paul singles out prophecy, tongues, and knowledge, underscoring their transitory, incomplete, and imperfect nature (vv. 8-9). Given this, these revelatory gifts allow the Corinthians only a partial understanding of the mysteries of God in the present. Unfortunately, the Corinthians pride themselves on their possession of such gifts and assume that they offer complete access to divine mysteries. However, complete access and

know partially; then I shall know fully, as I am fully known. ¹³So faith, hope, love remain, these three; but the greatest of these is love.

14 **Prophecy Greater than Tongues.** ¹Pursue love, but strive eagerly for the spiritual gifts, above all that you may prophesy. ²For one who speaks in a tongue does not speak to human beings but to God, for no one listens; he utters mysteries in spirit. ³On the other hand, one who prophesies does speak to human beings, for their building up, encouragement, and solace. ⁴Whoever speaks in a tongue builds himself up, but whoever prophesies builds up the church. ⁵Now I should like all of you to speak in tongues, but even more to prophesy. One who prophesies is greater than one who speaks in tongues, unless he interprets, so that the church may be built up.

⁶Now, brothers, if I should come to you speaking in tongues, what good will

---

understanding are a future reality associated with the end-time. When the *eschaton* arrives, these limited gifts will lose whatever partial significance they now have, since the perfect will replace and fulfill the partial (v. 10).

To illustrate his point, Paul uses an analogy (v. 11). As childhood values, behavior, and ways of thinking are abandoned as one matures into adulthood, so are the lesser or partial spiritual gifts abandoned at the *eschaton*. Prizing and boasting in partial spiritual gifts, just like prizing and boasting in certain ministers (see 3:1-4), again shows that the Corinthians are spiritually immature, despite their claims to the contrary.

In verse 12, Paul reinforces his point with one more analogical argument. Like indistinct mirror images, the insights acquired through temporal spiritual gifts are useful now but nothing at all compared with the perfect (face-to-face) vision promised at the *eschaton*. Faith, hope, and love are all hallmarks of Christian life in the present. Love is the greatest both because it is the supreme motive that allows Christians to use all the Spirit's gifts for the end toward which God has ordained them and because it alone endures eternal.

The use of spiritual gifts in the context of worship (14:1-40)

Having discussed the necessity of diverse gifts (ch. 12) and established love as the absolute criterion for evaluating the use of gifts (ch. 13), Paul now focuses specifically on the problems occurring at community worship deriving from the exercise of spiritual gifts. Apparently, those in the community fixated on speaking in tongues as a demonstration of spiritual superiority are causing chaos in the community. In chapter 14, Paul first unfolds a sustained argument for the desirability of prophecy over speaking in tongues (vv. 1-25) and then lays down instructions regulating community worship (vv. 26-40).

I do you if I do not speak to you by way of revelation, or knowledge, or prophecy, or instruction? [7]Likewise, if inanimate things that produce sound, such as flute or harp, do not give out the tones distinctly, how will what is being played on flute or harp be recognized? [8]And if the bugle gives an indistinct sound, who will get ready for battle? [9]Similarly, if you, because of speaking in tongues, do not utter intelligible speech, how will anyone know what is being said? For you will be talking to the air. [10]It happens that there are many different languages in the world, and none is meaningless; [11]but if I do not know the meaning of a language, I shall be a foreigner to one who speaks it, and one who speaks it a foreigner to me. [12]So with yourselves: since you strive eagerly for spirits, seek to have an abundance of them for building up the church.

Need for Interpretation. [13]Therefore, one who speaks in a tongue should pray

---

14:1-25 Argument in favor of prophecy

Paul's preference for prophecy is predicated on two main arguments enunciated in verses 2-5 and developed in verses 6-25. First, what is articulated through prophecy is directed to human beings and is intelligible to the entire assembly, whereas tongues are directed to God and are not intelligible to all (vv. 2-3). Second, prophecy builds up the community, whereas tongues is an exercise in self-edification (v. 4). In verse 5, Paul restates his points, insisting that prophecy is the greater gift, although he acknowledges that tongues could have edifying value if they are interpreted.

Paul develops his argument that tongues are unintelligible in verses 6-12. With the exception of verse 6, where Paul offers an autobiographical reflection, perhaps hypothetical or perhaps an actual comment on his strategy at Corinth (see 2:1), this subsection is constructed around three analogies (vv. 7-11). In the first, tongues are likened to isolated notes sounded by a flute or harp. Unless the notes form a coherent pattern, no intelligible melody is produced and listeners are at a loss. Likewise, if a bugle is made to emit a series of random sounds, troops would not know they are being called to assemble for battle. In this second case, the lack of intelligibility is not merely benign. Paul's third analogy turns on the variety of languages. When no common language exists to unite two people, they remain estranged, an unfortunate outcome. For Paul, speaking in tongues amounts to unintelligibility (v. 9), on a par with the three examples cited. Paul concludes by positively acknowledging the zeal of the Corinthians. It is good, but it needs to be directed toward acquiring the gifts that build up the whole community (v. 12).

The lack of intelligibility and its consequences are now considered in view of the community's worship assembly (vv. 13-19). Without the com-

to be able to interpret. [14][For] if I pray in a tongue, my spirit is at prayer but my mind is unproductive. [15]So what is to be done? I will pray with the spirit, but I will also pray with the mind. I will sing praise with the spirit, but I will also sing praise with the mind. [16]Otherwise, if you pronounce a blessing [with] the spirit, how shall one who holds the place of the uninstructed say the "Amen" to your thanksgiving, since he does not know what you are saying? [17]For you may be giving thanks very well, but the other is not built up. [18]I give thanks to God that I speak in tongues more than any of you, [19]but in the church I would rather speak five words with my mind, so as to instruct others also, than ten thousand words in a tongue.

Functions of These Gifts. [20]Brothers, stop being childish in your thinking. In respect to evil be like infants, but in your thinking be mature. [21]It is written in the law:

"By people speaking strange
tongues
and by the lips of foreigners
I will speak to this people,
and even so they will not listen
to me,

says the Lord." [22]Thus, tongues are a sign not for those who believe but for unbelievers, whereas prophecy is not for unbelievers but for those who believe.

---

plementary gift of "interpretation," for which speakers in tongues should pray, tongues do not edify. The Corinthians may feel that truly genuine spiritual experience transcends the human mind. However, Paul suggests that in some way their experience in the Spirit must be translated into what is intelligible with the mind, because only in this way is the community built up (vv. 14-15). Additionally, when intelligibility is lacking, community members cannot authentically participate in community prayer. They can say "Amen," but since they have no idea what they affirm, their prayer and praise are rendered inauthentic. In concluding, Paul claims that he could outdo any of the Corinthians when it comes to speaking in tongues (v. 18). However, he again sets an example of renunciation for the benefit of others, consistent with what he had recommended in chapters 8–10.

Paul now turns to his second concern: the effect of tongues and prophecy on outsiders/unbelievers. In verse 21, Paul cites Isaiah 28:11-12. An interpretation of this text then follows in verse 22, which states, in effect, that tongues are for unbelievers, while prophecy is for believers. In all probability, verse 22 represents the view of some Corinthians who claim that their dazzling displays of ecstatic speech would win over unbelievers. Paul challenges and corrects this view in verses 23-25, insisting that tongues negatively impact unbelievers, while prophecy brings them to recognize the presence of God. However we construe these verses, Paul's view is clear in verses 24-25: prophecy is also better for unbelievers.

²³So if the whole church meets in one place and everyone speaks in tongues, and then uninstructed people or unbelievers should come in, will they not say that you are out of your minds? ²⁴But if everyone is prophesying, and an unbeliever or uninstructed person should come in, he will be convinced by everyone and judged by everyone, ²⁵and the secrets of his heart will be disclosed, and so he will fall down and worship God, declaring, "God is really in your midst."

Rules of Order. ²⁶So what is to be done, brothers? When you assemble, one has a psalm, another an instruction, a revelation, a tongue, or an interpretation. Everything should be done for building up. ²⁷If anyone speaks in a tongue, let it be two or at most three, and each in turn, and one should interpret. ²⁸But if there is no interpreter, the person should keep silent in the church and speak to himself and to God.

²⁹Two or three prophets should speak, and the others discern. ³⁰But if a revelation is given to another person sitting there, the first one should be silent. ³¹For you can all prophesy one by one, so that all may learn and all be encouraged. ³²Indeed, the spirits of prophets are under the prophets' control, ³³since he is not the God of disorder but of peace.

As in all the churches of the holy ones, ³⁴women should keep silent in the churches, for they are not allowed to speak, but should be subordinate, as

14:26-40 Regulating community worship

The varieties of gifts spoken of in chapter 12 are evident when the Corinthians congregate for worship, which Paul here describes as a lively, Spirit-filled assembly of believers, each bringing some spiritual gift. To ensure that every gift, including tongues, is directed to its proper end, that is, the upbuilding of the community (v. 26), Paul proposes some rules of order. He first regulates the use of tongues, which some apparently exercised in an uncontrolled manner, monopolizing the community's assembly time and creating disorder. As a gift, tongues cannot be excluded, but Paul sets three controls on their use. He limits the number of contributions from those gifted with tongues, prohibits simultaneous speaking in tongues, and enjoins the speaker of tongues to exercise this gift in silence if there is no interpreter (vv. 27-28).

With regard to prophecy, Paul also limits the number of contributions to two or three. However, Paul allows that as many as have a revelation may speak, as long as no two speak simultaneously, so that each may listen to and learn from the other (vv. 29-31). These controls may sound reasonable to modern readers accustomed to ordered and decorous worship assemblies, in which everyone's place and time to speak are predetermined. However, some of the Corinthians who like to show off their spiritual gifts may perceive these controls as contrary to the free flow and spontaneous activity of the Spirit. Who is Paul to constrain the Spirit?

even the law says. ³⁵But if they want to learn anything, they should ask their husbands at home. For it is improper for a woman to speak in the church. ³⁶Did the word of God go forth from you? Or has it come to you alone?

³⁷If anyone thinks that he is a prophet or a spiritual person, he should recognize that what I am writing to you is a commandment of the Lord. ³⁸If anyone does not acknowledge this, he is not acknowledged. ³⁹So, [my] brothers, strive eagerly to prophesy, and do not forbid speaking in tongues, ⁴⁰but everything must be done properly and in order.

Paul seems to anticipate and eliminate this type of objection by reminding the community that God's Spirit cannot inspire any disorder or chaos, since God is a God of peace (v. 33).

At 1 Corinthians 11:5, Paul indisputably takes for granted that women pray and prophesy in the assembly. Is he now contradicting himself in verses 34-35 by enjoining silence on women, commanding their subordination to their husbands, to whom they are instructed to direct inquiries? Some commentators suggest that verses 34-35 are an interpolation (later insertion) dating from the late first century, more akin to the view expressed by the author of 1 Timothy as found, for example, at 1 Timothy 2:11-12. Others who take these verses as original offer a variety of suggestions. Some argue that male elitists in the Corinthian community, not Paul, held the view expressed in verses 34-35, which Paul actually challenges here, although no text evidence supports this suggestion. Moreover, it depends on an interpretation of verse 36 as a sarcastic rejoinder by Paul to the elitists. Some claim that Paul addresses only married women, though this distinction is not evident from the text. Still others argue that verses 34-35 contain Paul's real position, while 11:2-6 represent his concession to some women whom he allows to speak, but with restrictions.

Given the limited evidence, it may remain impossible to determine which suggestion accurately accounts for verses 34-35. In the end, the greater problem presented by these verses is not whether Paul did or did not write them, but how they are interpreted and applied. Responsible interpretation requires that these verses be considered in view of Paul's larger vision of church as the union of all men and women using their gifts and talents to advance the gospel of Jesus Christ.

As Paul concludes, he backs the Corinthian spiritualists into a corner (v. 37). Either they recognize what he has written (ch. 14 and maybe chs. 12–13) as a commandment of the Lord, or they are not the genuine prophets and spiritual people they claim to be. Then, without singling anyone

V. The Resurrection

A. The Resurrection of Christ

15 **The Gospel Teaching.** [1]Now I am reminding you, brothers, of the gospel I preached to you, which you indeed received and in which you also stand. [2]Through it you are also being saved, if you hold fast to the word I preached to you, unless you believed in vain. [3]For I handed on to you as of first importance what I also received: that Christ died for our sins in accordance with the scriptures; [4]that he was buried; that he was raised on the third day in accordance with the scriptures; [5]that he appeared to Cephas, then to the Twelve. [6]After that, he appeared to more than five hundred brothers at once, most of whom are still living, though some have fallen asleep. [7]After that he appeared to James, then to all the apostles. [8]Last of all, as to one born abnormally, he appeared to me. [9]For I

---

out, Paul announces the consequence for non-compliance (v. 38) before succinctly reiterating in verses 39-40 what he has argued in chapter 14.

ARGUMENT FOR THE RESURRECTION

1 Corinthians 15:1-58

Paul's last major argument of 1 Corinthians is a lengthy defense of the resurrection of the dead. As we have seen throughout this letter, exclusive concern for the spiritual and disregard for the physical underlie many of the behavioral problems Paul has addressed. In this particular argument, the focus is on errant thought not problematic behavior as Paul now considers the Corinthians' spirit-body dualism vis à vis the question of the resurrection. In line with their dualistic beliefs, it appears that some Corinthians consider eternal life an entirely spiritual existence, experienced apart from the body left behind at death. The paltry body has no place in this exclusively spiritual dimension of future existence (see above at 6:12-20), hence the denial of the resurrection of the dead (v. 12).

Against this view, Paul develops a three-stage argument. He first rehearses the tradition concerning Christ's resurrection (vv. 1-11). Next he argues for the resurrection in view of three factors (vv. 12-34). In the third subsection, Paul discusses the manner in which the dead are raised (vv. 35-49). He concludes this argument by affirming that the resurrection is a mystery apprehended through faith (vv. 50-58).

15:1-11 The resurrection of Christ: rehearsing the facts

Paul begins by reminding the Corinthians that what he preached to them was nothing other than the central gospel tradition concerning

am the least of the apostles, not fit to be called an apostle, because I persecuted the church of God. [10]But by the grace of God I am what I am, and his grace to me has not been ineffective. Indeed, I have toiled harder than all of them; not I, however, but the grace of God [that is] with me. [11]Therefore, whether it be I or they, so we preach and so you believed.

Jesus' death and resurrection, a tradition he himself had "received" and "handed on" (see 11:23). This tradition was articulated in an ancient Christian creed, which Paul now cites in verses 3b-5. The central faith conviction professed in this creed by the earliest Christians was fourfold: Christ died, he was buried, he was raised, he appeared.

Paul's recitation of the tradition serves two purposes here. First, it serves to remind the Corinthians that they cannot simply reject, alter, or hold a belief contrary to any of the foundational elements of the Christian faith. It is on this complete profession of faith, not just one or two elements of it, that they presumably took their stand. Moreover, it is through this faith that they and all believers are saved. If any aspect of this central faith conviction is altered or rejected, their faith would be in vain, a possibility Paul hopes to avert.

Second, the recitation provides Paul with the opportunity to introduce historical testimony to Christ's resurrection (vv. 5-8). This testimony is essential to his argument for the resurrection of the dead. It is important to observe that Paul insists that Jesus "appeared to" the witnesses, not that they saw Jesus. This is intended to underscore the fact that the risen Jesus was not a construct of the witnesses' imagination. Peter is listed as the first to whom Jesus appeared, a privilege that contributed to his status in the early church; then come the "Twelve," Jesus' inner circle of disciples, who exercised an authoritative and foundational role in earliest Christianity. The circle of witnesses widens as Paul mentions more than five hundred brethren, then Jesus' brother James, a prominent leader in the Jerusalem community (see Acts 15), then "all the apostles"(v. 7), obviously a reference to a group larger than the Twelve. Paul finally lists himself as the last and least of those to whom Jesus appeared (see 1 Cor 9:1; Gal 1:16; Acts 9:3-5). The autobiographical aside "as to one born abnormally" (v. 8; literally "born of an abortion") is a strange expression, probably inserted to emphasize Paul's exceptional route to apostleship.

Notably absent from Paul's list of witnesses are women, who according to all four Gospels (see Mark 16:1-8; Matt 28:1-10; Luke 24:1-9; John 20:1-18) were the first to witness to the resurrection. Whatever the reason

B. The Resurrection of the Dead

Results of Denial. ¹²But if Christ is preached as raised from the dead, how can some among you say there is no resurrection of the dead? ¹³If there is no resurrection of the dead, then neither has Christ been raised. ¹⁴And if Christ has not been raised, then empty [too] is our preaching; empty, too, your faith. ¹⁵Then we are also false witnesses to God, because we testified against God that he raised Christ, whom he did not raise if in fact the dead are not raised. ¹⁶For if the dead are not raised, neither has Christ been raised, ¹⁷and if Christ has not been raised, your faith is vain; you are still in your sins. ¹⁸Then those who have fallen asleep in Christ have perished. ¹⁹If for this life only we have hoped in Christ, we are the most pitiable people of all.

Christ the Firstfruits. ²⁰But now Christ has been raised from the dead, the firstfruits of those who have fallen asleep. ²¹For since death came through a human being, the resurrection of the dead came also through a human being. ²²For just as in Adam all die, so too in

---

for the omission, which is a matter of speculation, Paul has compiled what he considers to be a list of witnesses sufficient to verify that Jesus who died and was buried was indeed raised from the dead!

15:12-34 The reality of the resurrection of the dead

Paul now moves to the specific controversy in the Corinthian community, which becomes explicit in verse 12: some deny the resurrection of the dead. To counter this claim, Paul advances three arguments in verses 12-34. First, he exposes both the logical inconsistency of their claim in view of the testimony to the resurrection and the chain of absurd conclusions one would have to draw if one were to reason based on the Corinthians' premise (vv. 13-19). In verses 13-14, Paul lists each of these conclusions. To reinforce his point, he restates the same chain of conclusions in verses 15-17 but in the reverse order, adding that the Corinthians would still be in their sin (v. 17)! Moreover, the dead in Christ would simply have perished (v. 18). With this first argument Paul sets out the devastating consequences of the Corinthians' claim and, as a final reinforcement, notes how utterly sham is their hope and how pitiable they indeed are if there is no future resurrection (v. 19).

Paul's second argument (vv. 20-28) begins with the attested reality of Christ's resurrection (v. 20), based on which he draws out the key consequence of this central gospel conviction for believers: they, too, will be raised through Christ. Paul illustrates this fact in two ways. First, Christ is the "firstfruits." The ripening of the firstfruits signaled that the rest of the fruit would also ripen and would soon be ready for harvest. Paul metaphorically applies this idea to illustrate that Christ's own resurrec-

Christ shall all be brought to life, [23]but each one in proper order: Christ the firstfruits; then, at his coming, those who belong to Christ; [24]then comes the end, when he hands over the kingdom to his God and Father, when he has destroyed every sovereignty and every authority and power. [25]For he must reign until he has put all his enemies under his feet. [26]The last enemy to be destroyed is death, [27]for "he subjected everything under his feet." But when it says that everything has been subjected, it is clear that it excludes the one who subjected everything to him. [28]When everything is subjected to him, then the Son himself will [also] be subjected to the one who subjected everything to him, so that God may be all in all.

Practical Arguments. [29]Otherwise, what will people accomplish by having themselves baptized for the dead? If the dead are not raised at all, then why are they having themselves baptized for them?

[30]Moreover, why are we endangering ourselves all the time? [31]Every day I face death; I swear it by the pride in

---

tion guarantees and heralds the resurrection of all believers (v. 20). Second, Christ is the antitype of Adam. Whereas through Adam death became the destiny of all, through Christ all believers are destined to life (vv. 21-22). Then, in language rooted in Jewish apocalyptic, Paul describes the events that will transpire at the Lord's second coming (vv. 23-28).

The resurrection of believers is a future event coinciding with Christ's second coming, not before. When the resurrection is completed, then comes the "end," that is, the fulfillment of God's salvific plan in Christ, which entails the subduing and destruction of all powers hostile to God and the establishment of God's reign. This work begun through Christ's death and resurrection will come to completion at his second coming. Every sovereignty, authority, and power (v. 24)—terms referring to hostile cosmic powers and perhaps more pointedly to the political leaders and corrupt structures of Roman Corinth—will be destroyed. Death is personified as the last enemy, the quintessential symbol of all resistance to God, since it is the lot of all those under the reign of sin (v. 26).

Christ must reign until he has subdued all these enemies and they are subjected to him. This idea is expressed in verses 25 and 27, where Paul alludes to and christologically reinterprets Psalm 8:7 and Psalm 110:1 to confirm the necessity of Christ's reign and his ultimate victory over all things, including death. While it is difficult to know whether by "him" in verse 27 Paul means Christ or God, the psalm allusions suggest that Paul intends that all is made subject to Christ through God, who is the One exempt from subjugation. Indeed, in the end Christ himself will be subjected to the One so that God may be all in all (v. 28).

you [brothers] that I have in Christ Jesus our Lord. ³²If at Ephesus I fought with beasts, so to speak, what benefit was it to me? If the dead are not raised:

"Let us eat and drink,
for tomorrow we die."

³³Do not be led astray:
"Bad company corrupts good morals."

³⁴Become sober as you ought and stop sinning. For some have no knowledge of God; I say this to your shame.

In phases one and two of his argument against the Corinthian denial of the resurrection, Paul first showed the absurdity of their denial and then established the certainty of the future resurrection of all believers, which is guaranteed through Christ's own resurrection. In this third step (vv. 29-34), Paul marshals two *ad hominem* arguments to complete his case against the Corinthian position. Paul first alludes to a practice apparently common among the Corinthians, namely, vicarious baptism on behalf of the dead. Though such a practice is not attested elsewhere in the New Testament, Paul's reference here indicates that it was a practice in Corinth. He does not opine about the value of vicarious baptism or inform us about the extent of this practice at Corinth. In view of his overall argument, he simply insinuates that the practice is useless if there is no future resurrection of the dead. By practicing vicarious baptism while simultaneously denying the resurrection, the Corinthians simply demonstrate their own logical inconsistency.

Paul's second argument concerns suffering. He continuously puts his own life in jeopardy and suffers for the sake of the gospel (see, e.g., 2 Cor 4:8-11; 6:3-10; Acts 18:23-40). Why would he do this if there were no hope of future resurrection? But Paul does suffer hardship, and this attests to the truth of the resurrection. Otherwise, he says, with a dash of sarcasm, the only wisdom to live by is that of self-fulfillment, which characterizes life without hope. This wisdom is encapsulated in the maxim Paul cites in verse 32, which was associated with the Epicurean school of philosophy. For Paul, this is no wisdom, because it fails to reflect the central Christian conviction that believers are destined to life through Christ. Paul concludes with sharp commands to the Corinthians to come to their senses. Citing a popular maxim attributed to the Greek poet Menander (v. 33), Paul warns the whole Corinthian community to stay away from those who deny the resurrection of the body. Since Paul has just cited the useless wisdom of Greek philosophy in verse 32, it may be that he is warning the Corinthians against dangerous dabbling in Greek philosophical ideas that subvert the gospel. If the Corinthians do this, they are not unlike those who are ignorant of God, that is, the pagans. Paul's concluding remark (v.

C. The Manner of Resurrection

◄ ³⁵But someone may say, "How are the dead raised? With what kind of body will they come back?"

The Resurrection Body. ³⁶You fool! What you sow is not brought to life unless it dies. ³⁷And what you sow is not the body that is to be but a bare kernel of wheat, perhaps, or of some other kind; ³⁸but God gives it a body as he chooses, and to each of the seeds its own body. ³⁹Not all flesh is the same, but there is one kind for human beings, another kind of flesh for animals, another kind of flesh for birds, and another for fish. ⁴⁰There are both heavenly bodies and earthly bodies, but the brightness of the heavenly is one kind and that of the earthly another. ⁴¹The brightness of the sun is one kind, the brightness of the moon another, and the brightness of the stars another. For star differs from star in brightness.

⁴²So also is the resurrection of the ► dead. It is sown corruptible; it is raised incorruptible. ⁴³It is sown dishonorable; it is raised glorious. It is sown weak; it is raised powerful. ⁴⁴It is sown a natural ► body; it is raised a spiritual body. If there is a natural body, there is also a spiritual one.

⁴⁵So, too, it is written, "The first man, ► Adam, became a living being," the last Adam a life-giving spirit. ⁴⁶But the spiritual was not first; rather the natural and

---

34c) sets recourse to pagan ideas on a par with recourse to pagan courts (see 6:5). Both are shameful!

15:35-49 The resurrection body

The two questions posed in verse 35 expose the basis of the Corinthians' qualms about the resurrection. They cannot understand how the dead are raised, nor can they imagine what a resurrected body will be like. In verses 35-49, Paul deals with the second question and leaves the other until verses 50-58. In his response to the question about the form the resurrection body will take, he employs a variety of analogies to argue that the resurrected body is a transformed spiritual body. Since a sown seed must die in order to become a full-grown plant, a fact that Paul presents as perfectly obvious to anyone capable of observing nature, the Corinthians are just plain fools to assume, as Paul implies they do, that a resurrected body is just a reanimated dead body (v. 36)!

Paul develops the seed analogy and through it establishes the crucial point that the sowing/fruition process is one that includes both transformation and continuity. The sown seed that must die does not come forth at harvest time as a reanimated seed; rather, it undergoes a radical transformation and continues its existence in a new and distinct body. Yet this body is necessarily organically linked to the seed because each seed transforms into a body peculiar to that seed (vv. 37-38). The mention of different

then the spiritual. ⁴⁷The first man was from the earth, earthly; the second man, from heaven. ⁴⁸As was the earthly one, so also are the earthly, and as is the heavenly one, so also are the heavenly. ⁴⁹Just as we have borne the image of the earthly one, we shall also bear the image of the heavenly one.

---

kinds of seeds with different bodies leads to a new analogy in view of distinctions concerning flesh (v. 39), and finally to another analogy based on distinctions between terrestrial and celestial bodies, each with its own peculiar manifestation (vv. 40-41).

The application of the analogies set out in verses 36-41 now begins with Paul's statement, "So also is the resurrection of the dead" (v. 42). The contrast/continuity between sown seed and full-grown plant is still at the basis of the four new sets of contrasting pairs now introduced: corruptible/incorruptible (v. 42), dishonorable/glorious (v. 43), weak/powerful (v. 43b), natural body/spiritual body (v. 44). The human person will continue in embodied existence, but as the contrasts make clear, the new body will be incorruptible, glorious, constituted in power, and above all a spiritual body, which does not imply some vague, ethereal existence but rather a body animated by the Spirit of God.

A new analogy built on an Adam/Christ contrast is introduced in verses 45-49 to further the natural/spiritual body contrast set out in verses 42-44. Paul begins with the observation that the first man was gifted only with physical, natural life (see Gen 2:7), whereas Christ was a life-giving spirit (v. 45). The one kind of body and existence that humans inherit from Adam precedes the other, spiritually animated existence that comes through Christ (v. 46). In and through Christ, the Corinthians will attain and live this completely transformed spiritual existence, but it is a future eschatological reality that must be awaited.

In view of the context, the contrast between "earthly" Adam and "heavenly" Christ (v. 47) should probably be understood as a restatement and reinforcement of the contrast already made between the natural life inherited through Adam versus the spiritual life inherited through Christ. Paul makes it clear in verse 48 that Christians are indebted to both the first and the last Adam. During their earthly existence, their likeness is to the earthly Adam; however, in their future eschatological existence in their resurrected bodies, believers will bear the likeness of Christ, whose resurrection is the guarantee of their own future resurrection. How will this happen? This first of the two questions with which Paul began this subsection at verse 35 is now taken up in the concluding section of chapter 15.

The Resurrection Event. [50]This I declare, brothers: flesh and blood cannot inherit the kingdom of God, nor does corruption inherit incorruption. [51]Behold, I tell you a mystery. We shall not all fall asleep, but we will all be changed,

15:50-58 The resurrection event

Paul's last section begins with a bold declaration that, at first, seems to play right into the hands of the Corinthians. Part of their problem with the resurrection is that they cannot fathom how anything corruptible and corporeal squares with future spiritual existence. However, Paul is not sustaining their argument. Rather, by underscoring the incompatibility of future eschatological existence with present existence, Paul actually argues for the absolute necessity of the resurrection. Without it, one cannot participate in future eschatological existence! But how will it take place?

The answer is a mystery, an insight about God's preordained plans hidden from the world (see 2:7) that Paul now unfolds in charged apocalyptic language and imagery. As Paul writes, he considers the second coming of Christ imminent. He and others ("we") who will not have died at the second coming, along with all those who are already dead in Christ, will be changed and resurrected into God-given spiritual bodies. Paul uses typical apocalyptic motifs and images (e.g., suddenness, the sound of the trumpet, awakening of the dead) to describe the end-time resurrection scenario. With the exception of the description of the Lord's arrival, Paul's revelation here is comparable to that found in 1 Thessalonians 4:13-18, the only other place in his writings where a revelation of this kind is unfolded.

In verses 53-54, Paul introduces a new metaphor to ensure that the Corinthians understand that the body will not be discarded or annihilated at death to give way to the eternal existence of the soul alone. He insists that the corruptible/mortal body will clothe itself in incorruptibility/immortality. Hence resurrected life will still be an embodied existence, but our flawed natural bodies will undergo a total transformation. When this occurs, the promise of victory over sin and death will have been fulfilled, not because of any human merit but because of what God has done in Christ (vv. 55-57).

Paul's concluding exhortation sounds rather general and disconnected from the whole preceding argument. However, it actually follows from the argument. The reality of the resurrection, which Paul has just argued in fifty-seven verses, is, in the final analysis, that which sustains Christians in their faith and their work of living and spreading the gospel. With this surety, neither their hope, faith, or labor is in vain!

⁵²in an instant, in the blink of an eye, at the last trumpet. For the trumpet will sound, the dead will be raised incorruptible, and we shall be changed. ⁵³For that which is corruptible must clothe itself with incorruptibility, and that which is mortal must clothe itself with immortality. ⁵⁴And when this which is corruptible clothes itself with incorruptibility and this which is mortal clothes itself with immortality, then the word that is written shall come about:

"Death is swallowed up in victory. ⁵⁵Where, O death, is your victory? Where, O death, is your sting?"

⁵⁶The sting of death is sin, and the power of sin is the law. ⁵⁷But thanks be to God who gives us the victory through our Lord Jesus Christ.

⁵⁸Therefore, my beloved brothers, be firm, steadfast, always fully devoted to the work of the Lord, knowing that in the Lord your labor is not in vain.

Paul's argument in chapter 15 is not a self-contained theological treatise on the reality of the resurrection but rather the culmination of all the preceding arguments in 1 Corinthians. Throughout this letter Paul has challenged the community to eschew behavior motivated by the ideas, values, and structures of pagan Corinth. As he now makes eminently clear in chapter 15, it is the reality of Christ's resurrection and the prospect of their own that constitute the moral compass that must guide and shape the Corinthians' lives. Their behavior must be compatible with the new moral order whose inauguration begins in the mystery of Jesus' death and resurrection and culminates in the mystery of their own resurrection, when God's purposes in history will be fully realized. The fact of the resurrection requires a radical reorientation of the lives of all believers, in the body, in the present, in anticipation of the future resurrection.

CONCLUSION

I Corinthians 16:1-24

With the major problems and issues of the Corinthian community now addressed, culminating in the extended discussion of the resurrection, Paul now brings up three final matters: the collection for the saints, his travel plans, and Apollos. Each is briefly treated in the first half of this chapter (vv. 1-12). In the second half of chapter 16, following the ancient letter form, Paul formally concludes this letter with a few exhortations and greetings typical of his own letter closings (13:23). In both verses 1 and 12, Paul begins with the formula "Now in regard to," first used at 7:1, which may indicate that his comments on the collection (vv. 1-4) and

VI. Conclusion

16 **The Collection.** [1]Now in regard to the collection for the holy ones, you also should do as I ordered the churches of Galatia. [2]On the first day of the week each of you should set

---

Apollos (v. 12) are responses to questions posed by the Corinthians in their letter to Paul.

16:1-12 The collection, Paul's travel plans, Apollos

Background information about this collection and the reason for it are not provided here. Paul assumes that the Corinthians know about this collection for the saints, meaning the Jerusalem community, as is clear from verse 3. Elsewhere, at Galatians 2:1-10, Paul recounts a visit to Jerusalem and his meeting with the church's leaders. After sanctioning his mission to the Gentiles, the leaders asked Paul to remember the poor, presumably of the Jerusalem community, which he said he was eager to do (v. 10). Thus the contribution for Jerusalem's poor, which Paul urged on all his Gentile communities, was apparently Paul's way of honoring that request. Writing a few years later in his letter to the Romans, he explains why the Gentile Christians ought to make this contribution. It is a debt owed by them to Jewish Christians, through whom they have become beneficiaries of Israel's spiritual blessings. Hence Jewish Christians should share in and benefit from the material blessings of Gentile believers (see Rom 15:27).

In addition to this express purpose, Paul may have viewed the collection as a way to foster unity between Gentile and Jewish Christians and to develop within the communities he founded a sense of benevolent regard for all believers everywhere. Paul's instructions, in line with those given in Galatia and presumably in Macedonia (see 2 Cor 8), underscore the fact that the collection was a part of Paul's missionary practice and not an imposition on this one community. At this time there was obviously no centralized system of collection in Corinth. However, no one was exempt from putting money aside privately and on a regular weekly basis, as clear from verse 2. Paul expects all collecting to be completed before his arrival, at which point the funds would be entrusted to the community's own appointees, whom Paul would provide with letters of recommendation, a common practice at the time to ensure the status of the envoys (see 2 Cor 8:16-24). Paul's final remark reveals his hesitancy to go to Jerusalem, although he apparently did go, bringing funds from Macedonia and the province of Achaia, of which Corinth was capital (see Rom 15:26).

aside and save whatever he can afford, so that collections will not be going on when I come. ³And when I arrive, I shall send those whom you have approved with letters of recommendation to take your gracious gift to Jerusalem. ⁴If it seems fitting that I should go also, they will go with me.

Paul's Travel Plans. ⁵I shall come to you after I pass through Macedonia (for I am going to pass through Macedonia), ⁶and perhaps I shall stay or even spend the winter with you, so that you may send me on my way wherever I may go. ⁷For I do not wish to see you now just in passing, but I hope to spend some time with you, if the Lord permits. ⁸I shall stay in Ephesus until Pentecost, ⁹because a door has opened for me wide and productive for work, but there are many opponents.

¹⁰If Timothy comes, see that he is without fear in your company, for he is doing the work of the Lord just as I am. ¹¹Therefore no one should disdain him. Rather, send him on his way in peace that he may come to me, for I am expecting him with the brothers. ¹²Now in regard to our brother Apollos, I urged him strongly to go to you with the brothers, but it was not at all his will that he go now. He will go when he has an opportunity.

In verse 5 Paul switches to a discussion of his travel plans. He assures the Corinthians that he will return to them, but not right away. He intends to stay in Ephesus, whence he writes this letter, to capitalize on evangelizing opportunities, notwithstanding opposition (vv. 8-9). The mention of Pentecost, a Jewish feast celebrated in late spring, places Paul's departure from Ephesus for the region of Macedonia in early summer. Only after visiting the communities of Macedonia, presumably at Philippi and Thessalonica, would Paul come down to Corinth to stay with them at some length, perhaps the entire winter (vv. 5-6).

After mentioning his own plans, Paul speaks of Timothy, who is apparently being dispatched by Paul to Corinth (see 4:17). Timothy's youth (see 1 Tim 4:12) and perhaps inexperience probably explain Paul's reminders to the community about how Timothy should be treated.

Paul concludes this first half of chapter 16 with the mention of Apollos, whom the Corinthians hoped would return to Corinth (v. 12). Some claim that verse 12 belies a real rivalry between Apollos and Paul and interpret Paul's comments as an attempt to dispel suspicions that he was obstructing Apollos's return out of jealousy. However, in view of Paul's description of the collaborative character of his relationship with Apollos at 3:5-9, it seems reasonable to take verse 12 at face value as an indication that there was no rivalry between the two co-workers. Whether Apollos ever did return to Corinth is not known.

◄ **Exhoration and Greetings.** ¹³Be on your guard, stand firm in the faith, be courageous, be strong. ¹⁴Your every act should be done with love.

◄ ¹⁵I urge you, brothers—you know that the household of Stephanas is the firstfruits of Achaia and that they have devoted themselves to the service of the holy ones—¹⁶be subordinate to such people and to everyone who works and toils with them. ¹⁷I rejoice in the arrival of Stephanas, Fortunatus, and Achaicus, because they made up for your absence, ¹⁸for they refreshed my spirit as well as yours. So give recognition to such people.

¹⁹The churches of Asia send you greetings. Aquila and Prisca together with the church at their house send you many greetings in the Lord. ²⁰All the brothers greet you. Greet one another with a holy kiss.

16:13-23 Concluding exhortations and greetings

With five terse exhortations, Paul begins the formal conclusion to 1 Corinthians. As he does elsewhere (e.g., 1 Thess 5:6; Rom 13:11-14), he exhorts the Corinthians to "be on guard," a phrase freighted with eschatological significance. The day of judgment is imminent, and eschatological urgency is the framework of believers' lives. Therefore, believers must be on guard for the arrival of the day of judgment and vigilant over their conduct as they await the second coming. "Be courageous" and "be strong" are rather general appeals, while the remaining two exhortations appear to be directed specifically to the Corinthian situation. By denying the resurrection, some were straying from the faith, in which, Paul now exhorts them to stand firm. The final exhortation that every "act should be done with love" recalls not only chapter 13 but the whole ethic of love and concern for others, rooted in the example of Christ, which Paul has sought to inculcate through his responses in 1 Corinthians.

After these brief exhortations, Paul singles out for praise some model members of the community who have used their gifts to serve the other members of the community (v. 15). He then exhorts the community to be "subordinate" to them (v. 16). This deference is not owed in view of any hierarchical office those praised occupy within the community. Rather, it is the witness of their lives spent in service to others that calls forth the community's respect and recognition (v. 18).

The passing on of greetings (vv. 19-20) is part of Paul's strategy to maintain communication between the churches and to reinforce the sense that all believers everywhere are joined in one new family of faith. Prisca and Aquila, who had arrived in Corinth shortly before Paul and offered him work (see Acts 18:1-3), are now living in Ephesus and are apparently

²¹I, Paul, write you this greeting in my own hand. ²²If anyone does not love the Lord, let him be accursed. *Marana tha.* ²³The grace of the Lord Jesus be with you. ²⁴My love to all of you in Christ Jesus.

---

leaders within the local church there. The greetings include a kiss, a public sign of the unity and reconciliation that existed among community members. The addition of the word "holy" (v. 20) need not imply that Paul has in mind here some type of greeting reserved for the liturgy.

Paul adds a postscript in his own handwriting, unusual with regard to ancient letter writing conventions and something Paul did only occasionally (see Gal 6:11-18), presumably to ensure his personal concern. Even more unusual in these final verses is the inclusion of a conditional curse (v. 22), which serves to reinforce the series of strict warnings Paul has already enunciated in this letter. The curse is followed by a prayer, *Marana tha*, "Come, our Lord," and then a typical grace benediction. Paul concludes with an assertion of personal love for the community, which is unique to this letter. This expression of love allows Paul to recall one of the letter's major themes and reinforce his own *ethos* as a loving, caring father, a powerful argument indeed for why the community should heed his advice, admonitions, and appeals.

The Second Letter to the Corinthians

Occasion and purpose

When we turn to 2 Corinthians, it is evident that the solid relationship between Paul and the Corinthian community, presupposed in 1 Corinthians, is no longer intact. Rather, the community's trust in Paul has eroded, and their relationship is seriously strained. Paul now finds himself in a defensive position, reflected in the letter's rhetoric, which is largely apologetic, struggling to win back the trust and esteem of the community.

Since there is no independent account of what precipitated this crisis and elicited 2 Corinthians, the situation must be reconstructed. A likely scenario based on the text evidence runs as follows: Paul had promised to return to Corinth for a lengthy visit after concluding his ministry in Ephesus and then visiting Macedonia (1 Cor 16:5-7) but did not do as promised. Rather, sometime after sending 1 Corinthians, he apparently changed his mind, deciding to stop at Corinth once on his way to Macedonia and again on his return from Macedonia, after which he would bring the Corinthians' collection for the poor to Jerusalem (2 Cor 1:15).

Paul did not follow through on these plans either. Evidently, he learned that the troubles in the Corinthian community had escalated, even though he had sent Timothy (1 Cor 4:17) and dispatched 1 Corinthians to deal with key problems. This troublesome situation was further exacerbated when rival missionaries arrived in Corinth. They discredited Paul and instigated a crisis between the community and him (2 Cor 11:4). To remedy the situation, Paul made an unscheduled, "pain[ful]" visit to Corinth, where he was publicly humiliated (2:5). Once back in Ephesus, he wrote the now lost tearful letter (2:4) and sent it to the community via Titus. Anxious to hear the community's reaction to this severe letter, Paul left Troas and met up with Titus in Macedonia (2:12-13). Titus reported that many in the community had realigned themselves with Paul (7:5-16), although doubts lingered about his trustworthiness, since he had changed plans and failed to make the promised visit (1:12–2:4). Apparently, others remained under the influence of the intruders, allied with them against Paul. In response to this situation, Paul composed 2 Corinthians.

The Temple of Apollo with the Acrocorinth looming in the background

Second Corinthians is our only source of information about the intruders. Paul's counter brag at 11:22, that he is as much a Hebrew and Israelite as the intruders, indicates that he regards them as Jewish Christians. Apart from this, Paul says only that they are "false apostles" (11:13) who preach a gospel different from his (11:4-5). They have "letters of recommendation" (3:1) and are supported by the community (11:7-12). They evidently boast about their rhetorical skills and knowledge (10:10; 11:6), appealing to their supernatural power (12:12) and visions (12:1) as proof of the superiority of their gospel and ministry.

Unfortunately, this information is too general, and probably too biased, to allow for a definite identification of the intruders. Though scholarly speculation abounds, perhaps the most that can be safely stated is that the intruders were Jewish Christians. Paul considers them adversaries and holds them responsible for having driven a wedge between himself and the community. As he tells it, they alleged that he was a frail and gutless preacher, forceful only on paper (10:1-18), deficient in speech (11:6), and without "letters of recommendation" (3:1-3). They apparently cited Paul's refusal of Corinthian financial support as testimony that he was no true apostle (11:7) and raised the suspicion that he was deceitfully intending to profit from the collection he promoted (12:12-16). Paul's failure to demonstrate the power of his message with miracles and signs and his lack of ecstatic visions (12:1-10) were also apparently evinced as confirmation of his inferior status.

The intruders were clearly attempting to dismantle Paul's apostolic authority and invalidate his ministry. They probably found a receptive audience among the spiritual elitists in the community, whose captivation with eloquent speech and boasting in ecstatic gifts and knowledge had already been a source of discord at Corinth (see 1 Cor 8–14). Although Paul reserves his most direct and vehement attack on the intruders until chapters 10–13, they are in the background of his argument throughout the letter.

The unity of 2 Corinthians

Scholars who claim that 2 Corinthians is a composite of letters or letter portions usually cite three blocks of text as evidence to support this claim: (1) 6:14–7:1; (2) chapters 8–9; and (3) chapters10–13. They argue that these text blocks differ so significantly from their immediate literary context in either content or tone that they must have been once-independent letters or pieces of letters occasioned by separate circumstances. Some would even argue that chapters 8 and 9 were each originally separate letters. Additionally, some maintain that at 2:13 Paul unexpectedly breaks his narrative, resuming it at 7:5. They point to the intervening material, that is, 2:14–7:4, as further evidence that 2 Corinthians is a composite. In view of these arguments, 2 Corinthians could be a combination of anywhere from two (chs. 1–9 and 10–13) to six letters or letter fragments.

However, the case for the composite nature of 2 Corinthians may not be as strong as it seems. First of all, the manuscript evidence supports the letter's compositional integrity. Second, as our study of 1 Corinthians has shown, digressions are not always signs of later insertions, nor does change of tone or topic necessarily signal a new letter or letter fragment. Third, when Paul's rhetorical strategy is considered, 2 Corinthians appears less disjointed and incoherent than is insisted by those who divide it.

Beyond these three observations, the fact that there is no scholarly agreement on the number of separate letters allegedly contained within 2 Corinthians is itself telling. Moreover, those who insist on dividing the letter are obliged to answer two crucial questions: What circumstances occasioned the writing of each presumably independent letter, and why were they stitched together to form canonical 2 Corinthians? So far the answers have not been compelling enough to warrant abandoning attempts to understand this letter as a coherent whole.

In its final canonical form, 2 Corinthians displays the typical features of an ancient letter. It has an opening section complete with name of sender, addressees and a greeting (1:1-2), and a blessing of God in place of the usual thanksgiving (1:3-11). The body of the letter extends from 1:12 through 13:10, after which there is a formal conclusion (13:11-13), with exhortations, greetings, and a benediction typical of Paul's endings of his letters.

From a rhetorical perspective, 2 Corinthians can be considered a defense speech (forensic rhetoric) within which Paul includes one hortatory unit concerning the collection (chs. 8–9). After the opening (1:1-11), Paul attempts to dispel doubts about his sincerity by clarifying the motives behind his change in travel plans and to showcase his good character in order to gain the community's good will (1:12–2:16). Then he goes to the heart of the matter—the defense of his ministry, which has come under attack. After dissociating himself from charlatans who peddle God's word (2:17), Paul follows with a series of arguments that underscore the validity of his ministry and his apostolic authenticity (3:1–7:16). Having worked to win back the community's support and esteem, he feels confident enough to solicit the community with regard to the collection for the saints, a matter of great concern to him (chs. 8–9). Then he directly confronts those whom he holds responsible for exacerbating matters and instigating the crisis at Corinth. In four stinging chapters, Paul attacks the intruders, unfavorably comparing their ministry and motives to his own to show that they, not he, are the real charlatans (2 Cor 10–13:10). After this climactic counter-attack, there follows a standard epistolary conclusion (13:11-13).

Key theological ideas

The First Letter to the Corinthians focused on various colorful problems pertaining to life in the community and community life in relation to the world outside. In contrast, 2 Corinthians focuses almost exclusively on the issue of legitimate Christian apostleship and the true character of ministry in the service of the gospel. Paul's understanding of apostleship is rooted in his theology of the gospel, specifically in the dialectic between weakness and power (see 1 Cor 1:18-31), which he applies to his own life and ministry. In his abundant suffering, Paul shares in the sufferings of Christ (2 Cor 1:5), and in his own afflicted body he carries about the dying of Jesus (4:10-11). These sufferings do not undermine his apostolic legitimacy but authenticate it, since it is precisely through weakness and suffering that God's divine power to save is made manifest (4:7). That is why Paul never attempts to overcome his weakness or shrink from suffering; rather, he boasts in it (see 11:30; 12:5), since it indisputably distinguishes him as a true minister of the glorious new covenant in Christ (2:14) through whom God has reconciled the world, inaugurating the new creation (5:11-21). In addition to his suffering, Paul also points to his sincerity (2:17), his willingness to forgive (2:10), his selfless concern for the Corinthians (12:11-18), and his moral integrity (8:20-21). All are a piece of the cruciform existence that characterizes the apostle's life and distinguishes and authenticates Paul as a true minister of the gospel.

This same cruciform existence must be the hallmark of every Christian life. Paul does not recommend weakness, suffering, death, or poverty to the Corinthians as ends in themselves (see 1:3-6; 4:10-12; 8:8-15). Rather, he insists that receptivity to the gospel message, the story of God's power and glory paradoxically manifested in Christ crucified, is demonstrated in one's acceptance of suffering, one's glorying in weakness, and one's selfless service to others for the sake of Christ, whose love constrains us to live no longer for ourselves (2 Cor 5:14-15).

OUTLINE OF SECOND CORINTHIANS

1:1-1	*Introduction*
1:1-2	Greeting
1:3-11	Blessing
1:12–2:16	*Paul's True Motives and Character*
1:12-14	Paul is sincere and reliable
1:15–2:4	The motives for Paul's change in travel plans
2:5-11	The fate of the offender
2:12-16	A positive outcome
2:17– 7:16	*Paul Defends His Ministry*
2:17–4:6	Ministers of a new covenant
4:7–5:10	A ministry of affliction
5:11– 6:10	A ministry of reconciliation
6:11-13	A personal appeal to the Corinthians
6:14–7:1	A call to holiness
7:2-4	Paul resumes his appeal
7:5-16	Paul's complete confidence in the Corinthians
8:1–9:15	*The Collection for Jerusalem*
8:1-8	The example of the Macedonians
8: 9-15	Motives for giving
8:16–9:5	Titus, his collaborators, and the collection drive at Corinth
9:6-15	The rewards of giving
10:1–13:10	*Paul's Counterattack on the Intruders*
10:1-18	Paul refutes his opponents' accusations
10:1-11	Spiritual weapons
10:12-18	Paul boasts in his own labors
11:1–12:10	The "fool's speech"
11:1-21a	A "little foolishness"
11:21b–12:10	Paul's foolish boasting
12:11-21	Epilogue and transition
13:1-10	Final warnings
13:11-13	*Epistolary Conclusion*

The Second Letter to the Corinthians

I. Address

◄ **1** **Greeting.** ¹Paul, an apostle of Christ Jesus by the will of God, and Timothy our brother, to the church of God that is in Corinth, with all the holy ones throughout Achaia: ²grace to you and peace from God our Father and the Lord Jesus Christ.

Thanksgiving. ³Blessed be the God ► and Father of our Lord Jesus Christ, the

---

INTRODUCTION

2 Corinthians 1:1-11

1:1-2 Greeting

Paul's self-identification as an apostle of Christ Jesus by God's will underscores the authoritative basis of his ministry, which is the result of God's initiative. Timothy, who had evangelized with Paul at Corinth (1:19), is mentioned as co-sender of this letter. Whether this implies co-author is not certain. The letter is addressed to the "church of God . . . in Corinth." The addition of "with all the holy ones throughout Achaia" allows Paul to accent universality, as he did at 1 Corinthians 1:2. Given the Corinthians' behavior, the designation "holy ones" seems ill-fit. However, this is their vocation (1 Cor 1:2), of which Paul again reminds them. The salutation, where Paul typically combines Greek *charis* (grace) and Hebrew *shalom* (peace), expresses his understanding of God's generous gifting of humanity with and through Christ and the well being or *shalom* that results.

1:3-11 Blessing

Paul begins with a typical Jewish benediction (vv. 3-4), blessing God who graciously comforts him in all his afflictions. Paul turns this experi-

---

► This symbol indicates a cross reference number in the *Catechism of the Catholic Church*. See page 151 for number citations.

A temple in ruins

Father of compassion and God of all encouragement, [4]who encourages us in our every affliction, so that we may be able to encourage those who are in any affliction with the encouragement with which we ourselves are encouraged by God. [5]For as Christ's sufferings overflow to us, so through Christ does our encouragement also overflow. [6]If we are afflicted, it is for your encouragement and salvation; if we are encouraged, it is for your encouragement, which enables you to endure the same sufferings that we suffer. [7]Our hope for you is firm, for we know that as you share in the sufferings, you also share in the encouragement.

---

ence into an opportunity to comfort others, becoming the conduit of God's comfort for those in need. Though the blessing proper does not extend beyond these two verses, two key terms, "affliction" and "encouragement" (Greek: *paraklēsis,* also rendered "encouragement" or "consolation") are repeated in verses 5-7. Here the focus is on Paul's relationship with the community, and the general notion of affliction is now subsumed under Christ's sufferings. As co-participants in Christ's sufferings, Paul and the community are bound to each other. Although Paul's share of Christ's suffering is "overflowing" (v. 5), he accepts this in view of its positive benefit for other Christians who must also endure suffering.

In verses 8-11, Paul concludes by appealing to the Corinthians for their prayers, reminding them of sufferings he endured in Asia, which left him so despairing that he had resigned himself to death. Beyond speculation that Paul here alludes to some experience in Ephesus (see, e.g., 1 Cor 15:32; Acts 19:23-40), it is impossible to know, based on the scant text information, to what traumatic experience he refers. Nonetheless, Paul makes clear that the experience did not nullify his faith. Rather, it resulted in his complete reliance on God and a more profound faith that, in the future, God would rescue him from death through the resurrection.

Why Paul begins with this blessing of God and emphasis on his suffering needs to be considered within the context of the whole argument he unfolds in this letter. As noted, the rival apostles had apparently cited Paul's suffering and weakness as evidence of his inferiority. Rather than deny his suffering, Paul subverts this criticism by identifying his suffering as a participation in the sufferings of Christ. Paul is not incapacitated by it; on the contrary, his suffering enables him to act as an agent of comfort to community members in their time of affliction. Suffering, the common lot of Paul and the community, cannot be a source of alienation between them, since their co-participation in Christ's suffering bonds them further to each other. Moreover, suffering has brought Paul to a more complete re-

⁸We do not want you to be unaware, brothers, of the affliction that came to us in the province of Asia; we were utterly weighed down beyond our strength, so that we despaired even of life. ⁹Indeed, we had accepted within ourselves the sentence of death, that we might trust not in ourselves but in God who raises the dead. ¹⁰He rescued us from such great danger of death, and he will continue to rescue us; in him we have put our hope [that] he will also rescue us again, ¹¹as you help us with prayer, so that thanks may be given by many on our behalf for the gift granted us through the prayers of many.

---

liance on God and has increased his hope in God. What could be wrong with the apostle's suffering? Clearly, nothing!

It is important to underscore that Paul does not promote suffering as an absolute good but values his suffering insofar as it serves his ministry. Indeed, it is in Paul's "overflowing" suffering, identified with Christ's suffering, that God's saving grace overflows and not, as the rivals would have the Corinthians believe, in demonstrations of power! Thus suffering cannot be discounted as a mere sign of weakness, and the Corinthians, far from taking offense at Paul's suffering, should bless God too! They should see in it the degree to which God is at work in Paul and find in his suffering both a source of comfort and union between themselves and their apostle, whose ministry they are called to share and support through prayer (v. 11).

PAUL'S TRUE MOTIVES AND CHARACTER

2 Corinthians 1:12–2:16

Circumscribed within the accusations brought against Paul by the outsiders and the larger controversy they have instigated is the community's own questioning of Paul's sincerity in view of his apparent failure to keep his word and visit them. If not addressed, this issue risks being magnified by the larger controversy. Therefore, before Paul tackles the major bone of contention raised by the intruders, that is, the legitimacy of his apostleship (v. 17), he first deals with this issue to make sure he has the community on his side. Paul begins by boasting of his sincerity especially toward the community (1:12-14). After showing that he has legitimate motives for foregoing his promised visit (1:15–2:4), Paul returns to the fate of the offender (2:5-11) before giving thanks for the positive outcome to this particular crisis and posing a final question that provides the opening for Paul to defend his ministry before the Corinthian community (2:12-16).

II. The Crisis between Paul and the Corinthians

A. Past Relationships

Paul's Sincerity and Constancy. [12]For our boast is this, the testimony of our conscience that we have conducted ourselves in the world, and especially toward you, with the simplicity and sincerity of God, [and] not by human wisdom but by the grace of God. [13]For we write you nothing but what you can read and understand, and I hope that you will understand completely, [14]as you have come to understand us partially, that we are your boast as you also are ours, on the day of [our] Lord Jesus.

[15]With this confidence I formerly intended to come to you so that you might receive a double favor, [16]namely, to go by way of you to Macedonia, and then to come to you again on my return from Macedonia, and have you send me on my way to Judea. [17]So when I intended this, did I act lightly? Or do I make my plans according to human considerations, so that with me it is "yes, yes" and "no, no"? [18]As God is faithful, our word to you is not "yes" and "no." [19]For the Son of God, Jesus Christ, who was proclaimed to you by us, Silvanus and Timothy and me, was not "yes" and "no," but "yes" has been in him. [20]For however many are the promises of God, their Yes is in him; therefore, the Amen from us also goes through him to God for glory. [21]But the one who gives us security with you in Christ and who anointed us is God; [22]he has also put his seal upon us and given the Spirit in our hearts as a first installment.

Paul's Change of Plan. [23]But I call upon God as witness, on my life, that it is to spare you that I have not yet gone

---

1:12-14 Paul is sincere and reliable

In verses 12-14 Paul transitions from the opening blessing but keeps the focus on the mutually beneficial relationship between himself and the community, boasting of his candid and sincere conduct "especially toward you"(v. 12). Paul is certain of this because what he says and writes he does by the "grace of God," that is, as one divinely commissioned to reveal God's wisdom in a completely intelligible way (v. 13). Not only can the Corinthians put away their doubts, but they can enjoy with Paul a relationship of mutual understanding and pride that will grow until "the day of [our] Lord Jesus" (v. 14). The benefit to the community accruing from Paul's sincere and candid preaching of the gospel justifies Paul's boasting and the community's boasting in him. This clearly distinguishes Paul from the false preachers, whose ministry is a vehicle for self-promotion.

1:15–2:4 The motives for Paul's change in travel plans

At issue here is Paul's failure to go forward with his planned double visit to Corinth (v. 16). He had not followed through on previously announced travel plans (1 Cor 16:5) nor on his new modified plans. The Co-

to Corinth. ²⁴Not that we lord it over your faith; rather, we work together for your joy, for you stand firm in the faith. 2 ¹For I decided not to come to you again in painful circumstances. ²For if I inflict pain upon you, then who is there to cheer me except the one pained by me? ³And I wrote as I did so that when I came I might not be pained by those in whom I should have rejoiced, confident about all of you that my joy is that of all of you. ⁴For out of much affliction and anguish of heart I wrote to you with many tears, not that you might be pained but that you might know the abundant love I have for you.

The Offender. ⁵If anyone has caused pain, he has caused it not to me, but in

---

rinthians are understandably irked and have begun to wonder whether Paul can be trusted.

In response, Paul offers two reasons for his change of plans. The first is unfolded in verses 15-22, where Paul begins with the positive statement that the purpose of the visit was to be of benefit (a double favor) to the community (v. 15), something with which the Corinthians presumably agree. Then in verse 17 Paul poses two questions, to which some Corinthians were likely to respond yes! Yes, you did act lightly! Yes, you are a vacillator, saying yes one day and no the next day! But Paul insists on his trustworthiness, which is guaranteed in view of two certainties: God's faithfulness (v. 18) and the constancy of Jesus (vv. 19-20). If Paul is commissioned by God who is faithful to preach the gospel of the Son of God who is ever constant, then Paul, too, must be trustworthy. Thus, the source of Paul's commission and the very commission with which he is entrusted both demand and attest to his own constancy and not simply with regard to his travel plans. The Corinthians should have no problem agreeing with this, since, as Paul reminds them, when they say "Amen," a reference to a liturgical formula, they put their faith in Christ in whom all the promises of God are fulfilled and thereby ultimately express their faith in the constancy of God.

Paul presents the second motive for his change of travel plans in 1:23–2:4. Not only is Paul constant, he is also pastorally concerned for the community with which he is bound in Christ through his apostolic commissioning (v. 21). Since his work is to advance the community's joy (1:24), and they his, the Corinthians should realize that Paul had their best interests at heart when he decided to forego another potentially painful visit (2:1). Instead, Paul substituted the planned visit with a letter, (the now lost "painful" or "tearful" letter), the purpose of which was to express his "abundant love" for the community (2:4).

some measure (not to exaggerate) to all of you. ⁶This punishment by the majority is enough for such a person, ⁷so that on the contrary you should forgive and encourage him instead, or else the person may be overwhelmed by excessive pain. ⁸Therefore, I urge you to reaffirm your love for him. ⁹For this is why I wrote, to know your proven character, whether you were obedient in everything. ¹⁰Whomever you forgive anything, so do I. For indeed what I have forgiven, if I have forgiven anything, has been for you in the presence of Christ, ¹¹so that we might not be taken advantage of by Satan, for we are not unaware of his purposes.

Paul's Anxiety. ¹²When I went to Troas for the gospel of Christ, although a door was opened for me in the Lord, ¹³I had no relief in my spirit because I did not find my brother Titus. So I took leave of them and went on to Macedonia.

2:5-11 The fate of the offender

The disclosure of the second motive brings Paul back to the painful visit and the fate of the one offending him (2:5-11). Most scholars assume that when Paul made his unscheduled visit to Corinth to address the crisis, some community member publicly challenged his authority. The fact that Paul reminds the Corinthians that this act of effrontery was not simply a cause of personal pain but an offense against the whole body of believers at Corinth (v. 5) may indicate that some in the community did not see it this way at all. However, "the majority" apparently did and acted to discipline the offender (v. 6).

Although no details about the disciplinary action are disclosed, Paul interprets the action as a demonstration that the community is "obedient in everything" (v. 9) and now asks that they forgive the offender (vv. 7-8). Neither the offender's identity nor the exact nature of the offense is mentioned. Attempts to identify the offender here with the community member censured for immorality (see 1 Cor 5:1-13) have failed to convince for a number of reasons. For example, Paul's approach to the offender here is quite lenient in comparison with his severe posture toward the offender of 1 Corinthians 5. Moreover, the roles attributed to Satan in each situation are substantially different. At 1 Corinthians 5:5, Satan was to destroy the offender's flesh. Here at 2:11, Satan is a potential threat to the community if the offender is not forgiven. Since Paul elsewhere associates the false apostles with Satan (11:13-14), his concern here may be that the intruders/Satan will seize upon this situation to sow further discord within the community and between the community and Paul; hence Paul's recommendation to forgive and restore the offender to fellowship.

B. Paul's Ministry

Ministers of a New Covenant. [14]But thanks be to God, who always leads us in triumph in Christ and manifests through us the odor of the knowledge of him in every place. [15]For we are the aroma of Christ for God among those who are being saved and among those who are perishing, [16]to the latter an odor of death that leads to death, to the former an odor of life that leads to life. Who is qualified for this? [17]For we are not like the many who trade on the

---

2:12-16 A positive outcome

Paul now recalls how he had come to hear that the majority of Corinthians did the right thing and disciplined the offender (vv. 12-13). Having decided to send Titus to Corinth with the tearful letter, Paul went on to Troas to evangelize. While there, he was so distracted by his concern over the unfolding of events in Corinth that he aborted his evangelizing mission and went to Macedonia to catch Titus as he was returning from Corinth. Paul's relief at the positive outcome and his joy that the gospel was being advanced led him to express words of thanks to God (v. 14).

The metaphoric language introduced here touches on Paul's apostolic self- understanding, his role and his adequacy to perform that role, which he will defend at length beginning in 2:17. The first metaphor is drawn from the practice of triumphal processions in which conquering generals paraded their captives (v. 14). Here Paul's apostolic self-understanding emerges as he metaphorically presents himself as a captive paraded about by the victor, God. Paul, the itinerant missionary, is not at liberty to be self-directing (see 1 Cor 9:16-17). Rather, as a captive, dragged about by God, he exudes "the odor of the knowledge" of God in every place (2:14). The imagery of "odor" may derive from Sirach 24:15, where God's wisdom is referred to as a scent or fragrance. If so, then Paul presents himself as the shamed and afflicted apostle/captive who emanates God's odor/wisdom. Since Christ is the wisdom and, therefore, the true aroma of God, the apostles who proclaim Christ are indeed the "aroma of Christ" (v. 15) exuding the message of Christ crucified, God's wisdom. As one bound to fulfill this role, Paul acknowledges its serious implications. To some, through faith, what the apostle secretes will be the scent of salvation leading to life; to others, it is the odor of death leading to destruction (see 1 Cor 1:18). Paul's concluding question, "Who is qualified for this?" underscores how crucial the ministry of the gospel is. The question remains unanswered here, but the implication is clear. No one is fit for the task, save whomever God captures and equips to execute it.

word of God; but as out of sincerity, indeed as from God and in the presence of God, we speak in Christ.

3 ¹Are we beginning to commend ourselves again? Or do we need, as some do, letters of recommendation to

---

PAUL DEFENDS HIS MINISTRY

2 Corinthians 2:17– 7:16

So far Paul has attempted to allay doubts about his reliability, reestablish his good character, and regain the community's good will. All this paves the way for his engagement with the major point of controversy: the validity and authenticity of his ministry. Though the controversy is ostensibly between Paul and the community, lurking in the background of his comments are the intruders. Their arrival and style of ministry have precipitated the crisis, since Paul is being unfavorably compared with them.

Paul begins by refuting a double charge and launches the first step of his defense, which is built around the contrast between his and Moses' ministry (2:17– 4:6). Having established the superiority of the ministry of glory with which he is entrusted, Paul argues that this ministry is characterized by afflictions that, paradoxically, constitute the credentials of a true apostle (4:7–5:10). He continues the characterization of his ministry as one of reconciliation (5:11–6:10), which climaxes with a personal appeal to the Corinthians (6:11-13). At this point Paul introduces a brief digression (6:14–7:1) before resuming his appeal (7:2-4), after which he expresses his complete confidence in the community (7:5-16).

2:17–4:6 Ministers of a new covenant

Based on his opening statements, it appears that two charges were laid against Paul, both relating to the validity of his ministry: one concerned his refusal of financial support (2:17); the other, letters of recommendation (3:1). As already discussed, the financing of teachers and preachers by well-to-do patrons was customary in Paul's day. Though Paul accepted financial patronage from some congregations (see Phil 4:16; 2 Cor 11:9), his refusal of Corinthian support (1 Cor 9:1-18) galled this community. Besides suspecting Paul of hypocrisy, the Corinthians were evidently not convinced by his argument that the nature of the gospel demanded that it be preached gratis (1 Cor 9:15-18). They operated with the notion that only paid ministers were quality ministers who could be expected to give their all (see 12:13 and 11:7-12). To make matters worse, Paul lacked "letters of recommendation." In antiquity, great value was placed on the testi-

you or from you? [2]You are our letter, written on our hearts, known and read by all, [3]shown to be a letter of Christ administered by us, written not in ink but by the Spirit of the living God, not on tablets of stone but on tablets that are hearts of flesh.

[4]Such confidence we have through Christ toward God. [5]Not that of ourselves we are qualified to take credit for

---

mony of authoritative figures who vouched for others' credentials through letters. Paul knew the importance of this social convention and, when necessary, could invoke his own authority to recommend others (see Rom 16:1 and 1 Cor 16:3).

In response to the first charge, Paul berates financed ministers as hucksters who "trade on the word of God" (2:17). He dissociates from them, contrasting their profit-driven ministry with his own, which is carried on in sincerity, to which God witnesses. For Paul, this is sufficient. As for letters of recommendation, here, too, Paul distinguishes himself from "others." That he would need to provide such credentials "again" is preposterous, as his question underscores (3:1), precisely because his relationship with this community, metaphorically referred to as a letter that Paul carries about in his heart for all to read, testifies to the authenticity of his ministry. This letter/relationship owes its origin to Christ and pertains to the new covenant, powered by the Spirit and written on hearts of flesh (see Jer 31:33; Ezek 11:19; 36:26), of which Paul is a minister. He would not be adequate to the task except that God has qualified him for it; hence he takes no credit—perhaps in contrast to "some others"—for the success of his ministry, which is "not of letter but of spirit" (3:6).

The contrast introduced here is not between a spiritual reading of the Old Testament versus a literal one, as often assumed, but between two possible principles by which the new covenant is to be animated: the Mosaic law, which drove the old covenant but brought death, or the Spirit who gives life (v. 6b). This contrast, in which the law is deprecated and by extension the entire old covenant, raises questions about God's purposes in giving the law, which Paul does not pursue here. Instead, he goes forward with the old/new antithesis by contrasting his ministry with that of Moses. The contrast builds on Paul's interpretation of Exodus 34:1-4, 29-35, the account of Moses' ascent to Sinai to receive the stone tablets on which the law was engraved. A key element in this account, taken up by Paul in verses 7-11, is the glory of the Lord reflected on the face of Moses, which became so resplendent as a result of his encounter with the Lord that the Israelites could not stare at Moses unless his face was veiled. In

111

anything as coming from us; rather, our qualification comes from God, ⁶who has indeed qualified us as ministers of a new covenant, not of letter but of spirit; for the letter brings death, but the Spirit gives life.

Contrast with the Old Covenant. ⁷Now if the ministry of death, carved in letters on stone, was so glorious that the Israelites could not look intently at the face of Moses because of its glory that was going to fade, ⁸how much more will the ministry of the Spirit be glorious? ⁹For if the ministry of condemnation was glorious, the ministry of righteousness will abound much more in glory. ¹⁰Indeed, what was endowed with glory has come to have no glory in this respect because of the glory that surpasses it. ¹¹For if what was going to fade was glorious, how much more will what endures be glorious.

¹²Therefore, since we have such hope, we act very boldly ¹³and not like Moses, who put a veil over his face so that the Israelites could not look intently at the cessation of what was fading. ¹⁴Rather, their thoughts were rendered dull, for to this present day the same veil remains unlifted when they read the old covenant, because through Christ it is taken away. ¹⁵To this day, in fact, whenever Moses is read, a veil lies over their hearts, ¹⁶but when-

---

light of this, Paul reasons that if the Mosaic covenant, pejoratively termed the "ministry of death," was attended by such glory, albeit a glory destined to fade, then the ministry of the Spirit, a ministry of righteousness destined to endure, must be all the more glorious. Paul further insists that the greater glory of the new covenant has nullified whatever glory once attended the old covenant.

Confirmed in this hope, Paul contrasts his ministry, characterized by openness, with that of Moses, characterized by covertness, as symbolized by the veil. Paul claims that Moses donned this veil to keep the Israelites from acknowledging the abrogation of this whole old covenant, whose vanishing glory was visible on his face (vv. 12-13). Paul's aim here is not to charge Moses with deception but, as is clear from verse 14, where the veil becomes a metaphor for Israel's blindness, to impugn the Israelites for their hardened minds. Paul then transfers his remarks about historical Israel to his Jewish contemporaries, hardened still. Though Paul condemns them for failing to acknowledge that the old covenant is abrogated through Christ, he also appeals to them to "turn to" (convert to) the Lord, identified with the eschatological Spirit of freedom, which all believers experience (cf. Rom 8:2). Conversion removes the veil.

In verse 18, Paul reprises the key elements that have been part of his argument so far: veil, face, glory. Implicit in this verse is the contrast between the superior experience of all believers who pass "from glory to

ever a person turns to the Lord the veil is removed. [17]Now the Lord is the Spirit, and where the Spirit of the Lord is, there is freedom. [18]All of us, gazing with unveiled face on the glory of the Lord, are being transformed into the same image from glory to glory, as from the Lord who is the Spirit.

4 **Integrity in the Ministry.** [1]Therefore, since we have this ministry through the mercy shown us, we are not discouraged. [2]Rather, we have re-nounced shameful, hidden things; not acting deceitfully or falsifying the word of God, but by the open declaration of the truth we commend ourselves to everyone's conscience in the sight of God. [3]And even though our gospel is veiled, it is veiled for those who are per-ishing, [4]in whose case the god of this age has blinded the minds of the un-believers, so that they may not see the light of the gospel of the glory of Christ, who is the image of God. [5]For we do not

---

glory" and are progressively transformed into the image of God and the vanishing glory of Moses and the Mosaic covenant. In short, Paul has ar-gued that what the Spirit accomplishes in believers through the ministry of the Spirit, of which he is a qualified minister, eclipses the ministry of Moses, a ministry of law carved in stone, which was impotent to save. Though harsh in his denigration of the law and law-based ministry, Paul's views here are consistent with those he expresses elsewhere, especially in Galatians and Romans. It has been suggested that Paul's rivals in Corinth were Jewish Christians who insisted on the continuing validity of the law. Whether they in fact espoused this position is not certain. What is certain is that here Paul seems to refute such a view.

Paul wraps up this first phase of his argument by reaffirming that his ministry has its origin in God's mercy (4:1-6). Though the stakes attached to this ministry of glory are high (see 2:15-16), he is not discouraged. On the contrary, commissioned and qualified by God, he is a confident minis-ter of the gospel. He has no need to resort to deception and cunning, prac-tices he renounces as contrary to the gospel; rather, he ministers in openness and honesty, not compromising the truth of the word of God. This truthful manner of ministry, configured to the truth of the gospel, validates Paul's ministry and justifies his self-commendation.

Paul's admission that his gospel appears veiled to some (4:3) raises the possibility that his detractors accused him of being less transparent and sincere than he claimed. However, Paul denies that his preaching style leads to incomprehension. If some fail to perceive the light of the gospel, it is because the "god of this age" (Satan; 4:4) has blinded them. Paul knows himself to be above reproach in this matter because he preaches only Jesus Christ, in whom the light of the knowledge of the glory of God is revealed.

preach ourselves but Jesus Christ as Lord, and ourselves as your slaves for the sake of Jesus. [6]For God who said, "Let light shine out of darkness," has shone in our hearts to bring to light the knowledge of the glory of God on the face of [Jesus] Christ.

The Paradox of the Ministry. [7]But we hold this treasure in earthen vessels, that the surpassing power may be of God and not from us. [8]We are afflicted in every way, but not constrained; perplexed, but not driven to despair; [9]persecuted, but not abandoned; struck down, but not destroyed; [10]always carrying about in the body the dying of Jesus, so that the life of Jesus may also be manifested in our body. [11]For we who live are constantly being given up to death for the sake of Jesus, so that the life of Jesus may be manifested in our mortal flesh.

[12]So death is at work in us, but life in you. [13]Since, then, we have the same spirit of faith, according to what is written, "I believed, therefore I spoke," we too believe and therefore speak, [14]knowing that the one who raised the Lord Jesus will raise us also with Jesus and place us with you in his presence. [15]Everything indeed is for you, so that the grace bestowed in abundance on more and more people may cause the thanksgiving to overflow for the glory of God.

[16]Therefore, we are not discouraged; rather, although our outer self is wasting away, our inner self is being renewed

---

4:7–5:10 A ministry of affliction

In this second phase of his defense, Paul reflects on the paradoxical nature of authentic Christian ministry. Logically, the treasure, that is, this great ministry of glory, ought to be entrusted to a robust and resilient minister equal to the task. But it has been entrusted to Paul, weak and fragile as a common clay jar with a short shelf life. This paradoxical arrangement is not accidental but essential. Paul's weakness attests that apostolic ministry is powered by God and not the apostle, a fact borne out in the four antitheses set out in verses 8-9. In the course of his ministry, Paul survived potentially devastating adversities, not by the dint of his own inner resources but by the power of God. Paul's sufferings and weakness also attest to his union with Christ, whose suffering and death, Paul firmly believes, are being replicated in his own life of suffering and always with the paradoxical result that life triumphs.

This is evidenced among the Corinthians themselves. Life is at work in them, while, and precisely because, death is at work in Paul (vv. 10-12). However much Paul's suffering demonstrates God's power, affirms his union with Christ, and is the source of life for others—all good things— what ultimately makes his suffering bearable is the knowledge that he and all believers will be raised and brought into the presence of God and

day by day. [17]For this momentary light affliction is producing for us an eternal weight of glory beyond all comparison, [18]as we look not to what is seen but to what is unseen; for what is seen is transitory, but what is unseen is eternal.

5 **Our Future Destiny.** [1]For we know that if our earthly dwelling, a tent, should be destroyed, we have a building from God, a dwelling not made with hands, eternal in heaven. [2]For in this tent we groan, longing to be further clothed with our heavenly habitation [3]if indeed, when we have taken it off, we shall not be found naked. [4]For while we are in this tent we groan and are weighed down, because we do not wish to be unclothed but to be further clothed, so that what is mortal may be swallowed up by life. [5]Now the one who has prepared us for this very thing is God, who has given us the Spirit as a first installment.

[6]So we are always courageous, although we know that while we are at home in the body we are away from the Lord, [7]for we walk by faith, not by sight. [8]Yet we are courageous, and we would rather leave the body and go home to the Lord. [9]Therefore, we aspire to please him, whether we are at home or away. [10]For we must all appear before the judgment seat of Christ, so that each one may receive recompense, according to what he did in the body, whether good or evil.

Christ. This certainty is rooted in the belief Paul shares with the Corinthians that God who raised Jesus will also raise them (vv. 13-14). Verse 15 expands the thought of verse 12. Everything Paul suffers is for the community, so that the life that more and more of them come to experience will occasion praise and thanks to God.

Paul's firm hope in the resurrection and his present lived experience of inner renewal, even while his body is consumed by the rigors of ministry, bring him to affirm again, "we are not discouraged" (4:16; see also 4:1). In verse 17, Paul introduces a present/future contrast as he considers his sufferings in the context of the coming glory. By comparison with that future glory, eternal and weighty, Paul's suffering is light and momentary, further qualified in verse 18, as visible and transitory. Hence his focus must not be on his present suffering but on what is invisible and everlasting.

The mention of eternal glory leads Paul to reflect on his future destiny beginning at 5:1. This destiny concerns all believers, who are included in the "we." Paul's greatest desire is to be with the Lord permanently, which he speaks of as being at "home"(5:8). At present, he says, our "earthly dwelling," that is, the physical body, is a tent, a temporary home. When death destroys it "we have" (v. 1), Paul declares with certainty, a more permanent building, a spiritual or resurrection body awaiting us in heaven.

But how do believers exist between death and resurrection? For Paul, a disembodied existence, here negatively represented in the terms

The Ministry of Reconciliation.
[11]Therefore, since we know the fear of the Lord, we try to persuade others; but we are clearly apparent to God, and I hope we are also apparent to your consciousness. [12]We are not commending

---

"naked" and "unclothed" (vv. 3, 4) was unthinkable. Though he considers the physical body/tent a weight (v. 4), Paul does not want the disembodied, "unclothed" state that death effects, which can reasonably be taken to mean he does not want to die. Instead, he prefers that his body be "further clothed" (v. 4), in other words, progressively transformed until the mortal is swallowed up by life (see also 1 Cor 15:53-54). The Spirit is already enabling this progressive transformation from death to life (see 3:15; 4:16), guaranteeing (see 1:21-22) God's future and complete transformation of what is mortal. Until then, Paul acknowledges that the body is an obstacle to complete and permanent union with the Lord, who is known now through faith and not by sight in that direct face-to-face way that Paul desires (see 3:18 and 1 Cor 13:13).

This yearning for the Lord apparently outweighs Paul's misgivings about death as he now declares his preference to leave the body to be at home with the Lord. Paul's discussion of the impermanent, burdensome, and limiting character of the physical body could reinforce the view of some Corinthians, earlier refuted by Paul, that the body has no moral value (see 1 Cor 6:12-20). Here Paul concludes by pointedly reminding them that the Lord will judge each of them in view of the good or evil done "in the body," the only place where ethical behavior and moral purpose are manifested.

In this second phase of his defense, Paul has provided the Corinthians with a new framework for evaluating valid ministry and authentic apostleship. Within this framework, weakness and suffering necessarily, even though paradoxically, constitute the hallmarks of a genuine minister because the gospel is paradox. In Christ, God manifests power in weakness, glory through apparent shame, and brings life from death (see 1 Cor 1:18-30). In Paul, an apostle of Jesus Christ, God's glory and power are again made manifest in the apostle's weakness, sufferings, and death. The Corinthians are not only joined to Paul in suffering (1:7), but through his ministry of hardship they are already experiencing life.

5:11– 6:10 A ministry of reconciliation

At the end of the previous argument, Paul's focus shifted to the future of all Christians. Now at verse 11 he returns to his self-defense, beginning

ourselves to you again but giving you an opportunity to boast of us, so that you may have something to say to those who boast of external appearance rather than of the heart. [13]For if we are out of our minds, it is for God; if we are rational, it is for you. [14]For the love of Christ impels us, once we have come to the conviction that one died for all; therefore, all have died. [15]He indeed died for all, so that

---

a third phase in this long argument for the legitimacy and authenticity of his apostolic ministry. He addresses the community from beginning to end ("you," v. 12 and v. 20), though clearly with an eye to his rivals. Paul admits that his task is "to persuade" others (v. 11), yet he implicitly distinguishes himself from his rivals by emphasizing his transparency before God, which he hopes the Corinthians will also recognize. Despite his claim to the contrary, Paul is, in fact, commending himself, but not for selfish reasons. His purpose is to give the Corinthians reason to take pride in him, a man of substance (heart) and to rebut those who are all show, able to boast only in externals, perhaps even in ecstatic experiences (see 12:1) and miracle-working (see 12:12). Besides, as Paul makes clear, ecstatic experiences are private matters between an individual and God (see further 1 Cor 14:2). They are irrelevant to ministry, which is "for you" (v. 13). Paul provides this information to enable the Corinthians to make an informed choice between himself and his opponents.

Paul continues by appealing to the community's identification with the death of Christ and then draws out the implications of this event (5:14-17), whose universal significance is underscored in Paul's statement "one died for all" (v. 14b). How Christ's death benefits all humanity is assumed but not explained here. Rather, Paul is concerned to draw out the implications of Christ's death for all believers, about which the Corinthians obviously need to be reminded. First, all believers owe their new life to Christ and so must pattern their lives after his. Second, as a result of Christ's death, believers no longer belong to the realm of the flesh, that old existence of corruption and death that heretofore characterized human existence. Thus it follows that as those now "in Christ" (v. 17), the Corinthians can no longer know or judge Christ or anyone else "according to the flesh" (v. 16), that is, according to their old criteria.

Paul cites his own example to show how standards and values once considered important are now invalid (v. 16). Christ's self-emptying love is the basis of reconciliation and unity. This love has made possible the existence of this community, and Christ's love must be what compels the community to act and to judge. Since the Corinthians and Paul now know

those who live might no longer live for themselves but for him who for their sake died and was raised.

[16]Consequently, from now on we regard no one according to the flesh; even if we once knew Christ according to the flesh, yet now we know him so no longer. [17]So whoever is in Christ is a new creation: the old things have passed away; behold, new things have come. [18]And all this is from God, who has reconciled us to himself through Christ and given us the ministry of reconciliation, [19]namely, God was reconciling the world to himself in Christ, not counting their trespasses against them and entrusting to us the message of reconciliation. [20]So we are ambassadors for Christ, as if God were appealing through us. We implore you on behalf of Christ, be reconciled to God. [21]For our sake he made him to be sin who did not know sin, so that we might become the righteousness of God in him.

6 The Experience of the Ministry. [1]Working together, then, we appeal to you not to receive the grace of God in vain. [2]For he says:

---

from the same perspective in Christ and are expected to judge based on the same criterion, namely, Christ, it is clear that the community's negative assessment of Paul according to the old standards of power and prestige obviously needs to be reconsidered!

Believers belong to a "new creation" (v. 17), an entirely new order in which cosmic brokenness is now being reversed by the cosmic reconciliation willed and set in motion by God, who has "reconciled us to himself through Christ" (v. 18). Reconciliation is what God alone accomplishes through the agency of Christ. God, through Christ, rights the relationship between all creation and God's-self and all creation with itself, no longer counting believers' trespasses against them (v. 19). Paul is tasked with making known God's reconciling activity in Christ. However, he is no mere bearer of a message about a past event. Through his own ministry it is "as if God were appealing" (v. 20). Paul clearly understands himself as an agent of God's ongoing reconciling work, mediated in the present through his apostolic life and ministry. Thus he appeals to the Corinthians to be reconciled to God, which implies reconciliation among themselves and with Paul, God's minister of reconciliation.

Paul again directs the Corinthians' attention to what God has done in Christ, this time focusing on God's intention that believers "might *become* the righteousness of God" (v. 21, emphasis added). "Becoming" God's righteousness suggests that while God's salvific purposes are made known in Christ, believers are called to respond to God's offer by choosing to live out this righteousness. If so, a certain moral connotation seems to be attached to the notion of righteousness and needs to be manifested in holy

"In an acceptable time I heard you, and on the day of salvation I helped you."

Behold, now is a very acceptable time; behold, now is the day of salvation. ³We cause no one to stumble in anything, in order that no fault may be found with our ministry; ⁴on the contrary, in everything we commend ourselves as ministers of God, through much endurance, in afflictions, hardships, constraints, ⁵beatings, imprisonments, riots, labors, vigils, fasts; ⁶by purity, knowledge, patience, kindness, in a holy spirit, in unfeigned love, ⁷in truthful speech, in the power of God; with weapons of righteousness at the right and at the left; ⁸through glory and dishonor, insult and praise. We are treated as deceivers and yet are truthful; ⁹as unrecognized and yet acknowledged; as dying and behold we live; as chastised and yet not put to death; ¹⁰as sorrowful yet always rejoicing; as poor yet enriching many; as having nothing and yet possessing all things.

---

living. Knowing well the Corinthians' practical lapses both with regard to unity/reconciliation (see 1 Cor 1–4) and holiness (see 1 Cor 5–6; 8–10), Paul justifiably fears that the community has received the grace of God in vain (6:1). He therefore appeals to them to turn and respond to that grace. Though Isaiah, cited here in support of this appeal (6:2a; see Isa 49:8), envisioned the day of salvation as a future event, Paul believed that with the advent of the Messiah, that day had come. Salvation was a present offer, a grace to which the Corinthians needed to respond.

Paul brings the discussion of his ministry of reconciliation to a close by underscoring his own *ethos*. Neither he nor his co-workers has done anything to impede the Corinthians from responding to God's grace and fully partaking of this reconciliation. To reinforce his point, Paul briefly recaps how he has lived and worked among them. He has demonstrated endurance in the face of numerous difficulties (see also 4:8-10; 11:23-29; 12:10). Some hardships were inflicted by others (e.g., beatings, imprisonments); some were self-imposed (labors, vigils, and fasts). But Paul has not simply endured the hardships. He has acted with "purity," a reference to his selfless motives, and has demonstrated many other virtues (vv. 6-7a.) that attest to his authenticity as an apostle.

That Paul is able to withstand whatever befalls him is due to God who equips Paul "with weapons of righteousness at the right and at the left" (v. 7). The mention of the right and left could simply mean that Paul is fully prepared. In the context of the military metaphor, we should probably understand that Paul is prepared for both the offense and the defense, since the right hand wielded the sword and the left held the shield. Responses to Paul's ministry have alternated between extremes from glory

¹¹We have spoken frankly to you, Corinthians; our heart is open wide. ¹²You are not constrained by us; you are constrained by your own affections. ¹³As recompense in kind (I speak as to my children), be open yourselves.

Call to Holiness. ¹⁴Do not be yoked with those who are different, with unbelievers. For what partnership do righteousness and lawlessness have? Or what fellowship does light have with darkness? ¹⁵What accord has

---

to dishonor, from insult to praise (v. 8a). Whatever the response, Paul is prepared to fight whatever battles he must to spread the gospel.

Having once again demonstrated the authenticity of his ministry, Paul now introduces a final set of seven contrasts (vv. 8b-10), through which he deals with the negative assessments that have plagued his ministry. The first statement of each pair contains a negative evaluation of Paul, most likely reflecting the views of some in the Corinthian community. Paul simply counters each one by offering his own positive view of himself without adding any criticism of the Corinthians. The latter is unnecessary. In the end, the Corinthians' negative appraisal of their apostle shows that many are still attached to their former way of knowing and to judging "according to the flesh" (see 5:16). This again confirms their spiritual immaturity (see 1 Cor 3). If they were truly spiritual people, they would understand God's wisdom manifested in Christ crucified (1 Cor 1:18-31). With Christ as their standard of judgment, they would share Paul's positive assessment of his life and ministry, recognizing God's paradoxical wisdom at work in him.

6:11-13 A personal appeal

In a spirit of reconciliation, Paul now makes a personal and emotionally charged appeal to the Corinthians, in which he stresses his openness and affection for them and asks that they reciprocate by making room in their hearts for him. Rather than chastise the community, Paul speaks as a parent and guide to the Corinthians, whom he considers his beloved children in Christ (see 1 Cor 4:15).

6:14–7:1 A call to holiness

Having focused so far on his own ministry and relationship to the community, Paul now turns to the community's relation to the world outside. This shift in focus, coupled with the presence of some ideas and vocabulary not typical of Paul, have led many scholars to conclude that 6:14–7:1 is a non-Pauline fragment inserted by an editor. However, no manuscript evidence indicates an insertion here, and as many scholars

Christ with a liar? Or what has a believer in common with an unbeliever? ◄ ¹⁶What agreement has the temple of God with idols? For we are the temple of the living God; as God said:

"I will live with them and move among them,
and I will be their God

and they shall be my people.
¹⁷Therefore, come forth from them
and be separate," says the Lord,
"and touch nothing unclean;
then I will receive you
¹⁸and I will be a father to you,   ►
and you shall be sons and
daughters to me,
says the Lord Almighty."

---

now recognize, the passage is sufficiently Pauline in vocabulary and construction to be reasonably considered authentic. In fact, as with other Pauline digressions, closer examination often reveals logical links to the surrounding context. For example, at 6:1 Paul had already expressed concern that the Corinthians had received the grace of God in vain; hence this brief section in which Paul exhorts the community to recall its true identity and reaffirm its exclusive allegiance to God and Christ is entirely consonant with that concern.

Additionally, having just underscored his pedagogical relationship to the community in 6:13, Paul now assumes a teaching role at 6:14. He instructs and warns about alliances still maintained by some in the community that contravene allegiance to Christ and undermine the reconciliation achieved through Christ. This is especially evident in their strained relationship with Paul, God's minister of reconciliation.

Paul begins with a command that echoes the Old Testament prohibition (see Lev 19:19; Deut 22:9-11) against mismatching or, in the case of animals, misyoking pairs that do not naturally go together. The command is followed by six rhetorical questions containing six antithetical pairings: righteousness/lawlessness, light/darkness, Christ/Beliar, (an alternate term for Satan), believer/unbeliever, and the temple of God/idols (6:14b-16a). Through this series of questions, Paul again stresses the exclusive character of Christian existence (see 1 Cor 10:21). Implicitly, he exhorts the Corinthians to dissociate themselves from all that is pagan and to ally themselves exclusively with God, Christ, righteousness, light, etc.

Paul was quite aware that Christians would necessarily maintain contacts with unbelievers (see 1 Cor 5:9-10) and, in some cases, be married to them without necessarily compromising their relationship with Christ (1 Cor 7:12-14). Thus he cannot have intended here an absolute prohibition of all contact with non-believers. The point, rather, is that the believer's exclusive aligning of self to God in Christ necessitates the renunciation of

7 ¹Since we have these promises, beloved, let us cleanse ourselves from every defilement of flesh and spirit, making holiness perfect in the fear of God.

²Make room for us; we have not wronged anyone, or ruined anyone, or taken advantage of anyone. ³I do not say this in condemnation, for I have already said that you are in our hearts,

---

all activity involving alliances which compromise the believer's relationship with God and Christ and which defile the community, now identified as "the temple of the living God" (v. 16b). For Paul, the community constituted the spiritual temple of God in virtue of its being indwelt by the Spirit of God (1 Cor 3:16-17).

In verses 16b-18, Paul links a series of Old Testament references (Lev 26:12; Ezek 37:27; Jer 31:33c; Isa 52:11; Ps 2:7; Jer 31:9c) that underscore the reciprocal and exclusive relationship between God and the community. This radically exclusive relationship with God marks off true believers from unbelievers, whether within or outside the community, whose allegiance is divided. Moreover, it enjoins on each member of the community the obligation to be cleansed of all defilement in order to maintain the holiness of the community (7:1).

The function of this brief digression is to remind those in the community, probably the same spiritual elitists Paul criticizes in 1 Corinthians, that their continued courting of danger in pagan temples and their rabid pursuit of superficial, transient realities are at the heart of the problems in Corinth. They are responsible for compromising their relationship with Christ through the *koinonia* they establish with pagan idols in pagan temples. In their pursuit of external manifestations of wisdom and power, they show themselves attached to the conventions of the world and thus misjudge true ministers and misinterpret true ministry.

7:2-4 Paul resumes his appeal

Having implicitly inculpated the Corinthians for their tenuous relationship with Christ and near-ruptured relationship with himself, Paul resumes the plea begun above at 6:11-13, exhorting the community to make room for him. Once again he underscores his good faith toward them. He has not wronged, ruined, or taken advantage of anyone, in contrast, perhaps, to those who, in Paul's estimate, were taking financial advantage of the community (see 2:17; 11:19-20).

Though the Corinthians misjudge and malign Paul, he assures them that his intention is not to condemn them (v. 3a). On the contrary, as he

that we may die together and live together. ⁴I have great confidence in you, I have great pride in you; I am filled with encouragement, I am overflowing with joy all the more because of all our affliction.

C. Resolution of the Crisis

Paul's Joy in Macedonia. ⁵For even when we came into Macedonia, our flesh had no rest, but we were afflicted in every way—external conflicts, internal

---

has "already said" (v. 3b; obviously a reference to 6:11) and now repeats, he holds them in his heart, and his affection for them is so deep that he desires to die and live with them. Here Paul adopts, but inverts, a classic expression, "to live together and die together" (see 2 Sam 15:21) to articulate his own deepest desire to be fully reconciled with the community and share with them full partnership in the gospel. Despite the strained relationship with the community and the affliction Paul experiences, he expresses optimism that the Corinthians will reciprocate and that their relationship with Paul will be fully restored.

7:5-16 Paul's complete confidence in the Corinthians

Since Paul now picks up on points previously narrated at 2:5-13, many scholars assume that 7:5-16 originally followed on 2:13. Grammatically speaking, this position is difficult to sustain. Paul speaks in the first person singular ("I") at 2:13 and the first person plural ("we") at 7:5. If 7:5 had originally followed 2:13, why the switch from "I" to "we"? Additionally, certain vocabulary employed from 6:11 through 7:4 (e.g., affection, boasting, consolation, joy, distress), recurs in 7:5-16, suggesting more continuity between this unit and what immediately precedes it than is usually admitted.

Moreover, the claim that 7:5 is the direct continuation of 2:13 requires assuming either (a) that Paul abruptly broke off the story at 2:13 to focus on his own ministry until 7:5, at which point he just as abruptly returned to the thought of 2:13, or (b) that 2:14–7:4 is another original Pauline letter or letter fragment inserted here by a later, albeit inept, editor unconcerned about coherency! Assumption (a) implies that Paul was an erratic thinker/writer; assumption (b) implies that the letter lacks literary integrity. Both are drastic and, from the perspective of Paul's rhetorical goals and strategy, unnecessary.

It is important to bear in mind that at 7:5 Paul has reached a new point in his argument. So far he has carefully unfolded a defense of his ministry, which began at 2:14. At 8:1 he will begin his appeal to the Corinthians for money. The success of his collection drive clearly depends on the degree to which the Corinthians are well disposed to him. If they are not, Paul

fears. ⁶But God, who encourages the downcast, encouraged us by the arrival of Titus, ⁷and not only by his arrival but also by the encouragement with which he was encouraged in regard to you, as he told us of your yearning, your lament, your zeal for me, so that I re-joiced even more. ⁸For even if I sad-dened you by my letter, I do not regret it; and if I did regret it ([for] I see that that letter saddened you, if only for a while), ⁹I rejoice now, not because you were saddened, but because you were saddened into repentance; for you were

---

has little reason to hope that they will entrust their money to him, espe-cially given the misgivings they had about his sincerity (see 1:15-24).

To ensure that there were no residual hard feelings over the painful let-ter that could compromise his collection appeal and the continuation of his defense, Paul again focuses on the painful letter and his anxiety over it, which he only briefly mentioned at 2:1-13. Here, however, he speaks about the letter and its purpose, as well as his encounter with Titus, much more extensively and with new emphases. This elaboration of previously but briefly narrated points in the service of advancing one's argument at a later stage is an example of the rhetorical technique known as *amplificatio* ("amplification"). In its present position in the letter, this amplification functions as a hinge text. Through it, Paul continues and intensifies the optimistic line introduced at 7:4 and paves the way for his collection ap-peal in chapters 8–9.

Three smaller units comprise 7:5-16. In the first unit, vv. 5-7, Paul de-scribes the terrible state he was in at Macedonia before Titus came. The "fear" Paul experienced (v. 5) was probably due to his uncertainty about how the Corinthians would react to his "tearful letter" sent via Titus. Hav-ing written a stinging letter rebuking the community over the offense he suffered during his unexpected visit to Corinth, Paul knew that his letter had as much potential to alienate the community as it had to elicit their support and action on his behalf. Titus's arrival brings Paul a triple dose of encouragement (vv. 6-7). Beyond the joy of Titus's company, Paul is fur-ther encouraged to learn that Titus has not been rebuffed but edified by the Corinthians. The source of Titus's edification, the Corinthians' heart-felt concern for their apostle and remorse over the offensive incident, is the good news that relieves Paul of his anxiety and moves him to rejoice. As delighted as Paul is at this outcome, he is not insensitive to the pain he caused the community.

In the next unit (vv. 8-13a), Paul apologizes, but not without first dis-tinguishing between "worldly sorrow" and "godly sorrow" (7:10). Paul

saddened in a godly way, so that you did not suffer loss in anything because of us. [10]For godly sorrow produces a salutary repentance without regret, but worldly sorrow produces death. [11]For behold what earnestness this godly sorrow has produced for you, as well as readiness for a defense, and indignation, and fear, and yearning, and zeal, and punishment. In every way you have shown yourselves to be innocent in the matter. [12]So then even though I wrote to you, it was not on account of the one who did the wrong, or on account of the one who suffered the wrong, but in order that your concern for us might be made plain to you in the sight of God. [13]For this reason we are encouraged.

And besides our encouragement, we rejoice even more because of the joy of Titus, since his spirit has been refreshed by all of you. [14]For if I have boasted to him about you, I was not put to shame. No, just as everything we said to you was true, so our boasting before Titus proved to be the truth. [15]And his heart goes out to you all the more, as he remembers the obedience of all of you, when you received him with fear and trembling. [16]I rejoice, because I have confidence in you in every respect.

---

truly regrets the former, by which he means whatever momentary indignation the Corinthians experienced. But he does not regret the latter, because "godly sorrow" induces repentance, which is ultimately beneficial to the Corinthians (v. 10). It has awakened their sense of earnestness and an appropriate sense of indignation against the one who offended Paul, as well as their yearning to patch things up with Paul (v. 11). From Paul's perspective, the severe letter accomplished what he had intended, namely, that the Corinthians would show themselves truly Christian in the sight of God by their concern for his minister, Paul (v. 12). Thus Paul has good reason to be encouraged (v. 13a).

In the final subunit, vv. 13b-16, Paul again speaks of Titus. His success among the Corinthians was a source of joy to Paul, who had not lost face! The Corinthians had come through for him, having more than vindicated his boasting about them. All this joy and encouragement move Paul to express his complete confidence in the community (v. 16).

In this unit Paul has amplified the bare facts narrated earlier at 2:5-13, stressing every positive outcome of a situation that could have ended badly but, fortunately, did not. The Corinthians have shown themselves to be spiritually mature and have benefited from their repentance. Titus accomplished his task unscathed, returning to Macedonia impressed by the Corinthians' obedience and concern for Paul. Paul is encouraged and optimistic about his relationship with the Corinthians.

III. The Collection
for Jerusalem

◄ 8 **Generosity in Giving.** ¹We want you to know, brothers, of the grace of God that has been given to the churches of Macedonia, ²for in a severe test of affliction, the abundance of their joy and their profound poverty over-flowed in a wealth of generosity on their part. ³For according to their means, I can testify, and beyond their means, spontaneously, ⁴they begged us insistently for the favor of taking part in the service to the holy ones, ⁵and this, not as we expected, but they gave themselves first to the Lord and to us through the will of God, ⁶so that we urged Titus that, as he had already

---

THE COLLECTION FOR JERUSALEM

2 Corinthians 8:1–9:15

Having praised and flattered the Corinthians to the point of declaring his full confidence in them, Paul now banks on the hope, engendered by Titus's report, that mutual trust has been restored to press his case for the collection. The collection, for reasons already discussed (see 1 Cor 16:1-4), was of singular importance to Paul's gospel. If he has overestimated the Corinthians' good will, he could railroad his own cause. If, however, his optimistic assessment is correct, then this is the time to launch his appeal!

8:1-8 The example of the Macedonians

These first six verses constitute an introduction to Paul's argument. He is about to ask the community for money. This is never an easy task, and though Paul is hopeful that his reconciliation with the community is solid, he has to be cautious and avoid awakening any suspicions or hostile feelings. Thus he wisely begins by focusing on God, the Macedonians, and Titus. In this way Paul keeps himself out of the spotlight and lets the story of the Macedonian Christians rouse the Corinthians' emotions.

Despite their utter poverty, the Macedonians did not view the collection as an imposition but as a privilege through which they could express their fellowship with the "holy ones" (v. 4). They not only insisted on participating, but given the opportunity, they contributed "beyond their means" (v. 3) in a spirit of joy and generosity (v. 2). Paul attributes this abundant generosity not merely to the Macedonians' own goodness or sense of justice nor to anything he himself did or said, but to the grace *(charis)* of God (v. 1). In responding to this gift of grace, the Macedonians have shown their devotion to the Lord (v. 5). Their good example prompts Paul to urge Titus to go to Corinth (v. 6).

127

Mosaic of the head of Dionysus in a Roman villa

begun, he should also complete for you this gracious act also. ⁷Now as you excel in every respect, in faith, dis- course, knowledge, all earnestness, and in the love we have for you, may you excel in this gracious act also.

Whether Titus had been initially responsible for the collection drive among the Corinthians is unclear. There is no mention of him in conjunction with the collection instructions at 1 Corinthians 16:4. What we do know is that Titus had success among the Corinthians over other delicate issues, is purportedly well disposed toward them (see 7:7, 13b, 15), and is obviously equal to the task. By putting Titus in charge of the collection, Paul minimizes his own role and keeps himself in the background.

This story of the Macedonians' heroic generosity is quite moving and should have accomplished the desired effect of rousing the Corinthians' feelings of admiration or even envy, given their proud and competitive spirit. In either case, Paul has captured their attention and takes the occasion to exhort them not merely to participate in the collection but to excel in this gracious act *(charis)* of giving (v. 7). *Charis* can mean both "grace" and "gift" and is Paul's preferred term for the "collection." At verse 1 he used *charis* to refer to God's gift of grace given to the Macedonians, which enabled their own giving. Since, as Paul understands it, giving flows from being gifted, the Corinthians, who have been abundantly gifted by God, as underscored in verse 7, should naturally give freely and abundantly without being prodded. In fact, Paul refuses to mandate giving (v. 8), not because he fears their disobedience but because the gracious act/collection *(charis)* flows from the graces/gifts *(charismata)* received.

8:9-15 Motives for giving

Paul first relies on the example of Christ's own self-emptying gift *(charis)* to support his exhortation. His unique interpretation of Christ's self-emptying in terms of rich/poor is probably influenced by the current discussion and should not be taken as an indication of the historical Jesus' economic situation. At Philippians 2:6-11, we learn that Christ's self-emptying love demonstrated itself not only in the fact of incarnation but in the taking on the form of a "slave" and the subsequent total impoverishment that resulted from death on a cross. As a result of Jesus' self-emptying love, the Corinthians have been rescued from the poverty of alienation from God and restored to God's friendship (see 5:7-19). They are rich now. Paul proposes that they emulate Christ by manifesting their own love in their own self-emptying for the sake of enriching others. On a practical level, Paul would like to see this love be manifest in their participation in

⁸I say this not by way of command, but to test the genuineness of your love by your concern for others. ⁹For you know the gracious act of our Lord Jesus Christ, that for your sake he became poor although he was rich, so that by his poverty you might become rich. ¹⁰And I am giving counsel in this matter, for it is appropriate for you who began not only to act but to act willingly last year: ¹¹complete it now, so that your eager willingness may be matched by your completion of it out of what you have. ¹²For if the eagerness is there, it is acceptable according to what one has, not according to what one does not have; ¹³not that others should have relief while you are bur-dened, but that as a matter of equality ¹⁴your surplus at the present time should supply their needs, so that their surplus may also supply your needs, that there may be equality. ¹⁵As it is written:

> "Whoever had much did not have more,
> and whoever had little did not have less."

Titus and His Collaborators. ¹⁶But thanks be to God who put the same concern for you into the heart of Titus, ¹⁷for he not only welcomed our appeal but, since he is very concerned, he has gone to you of his own accord. ¹⁸With him we have sent the brother who is praised in all the churches for his preaching of the

---

the collection. Thus he encourages them to complete what they had already begun, assuring them that whatever they contribute, if properly motivated, will be deemed acceptable (vv. 11-12).

In addition to the example of Christ's love, which should be the Corinthians' primary motivation, Paul invokes the principle of equality as another motive for giving. Relatively speaking, the Corinthians are better off than the members of the Jerusalem community. Paul clarifies that he is not suggesting that the Corinthians disadvantage themselves (v. 13). Rather, by giving of their current surplus, they would be supplying what the poor lack. It is important to note that Paul does not advocate self-impoverishment as an end in itself but in view of fostering an equitable balance of goods necessary for living. He apparently intends that this principle of equality will be an ever-present motivating factor in all Christian communities, since he assures the Corinthians that if they were to fall on hard times, their needs would likewise be met in view of this same principle (v. 14). The citation from Exodus 16:18 recalls the distribution of manna in the desert according to need and serves to illustrate and support Paul's point (v. 15).

8:16–9:5 Titus, his collaborators, and the collection drive at Corinth

Paul now discloses the practical steps that will be taken to ensure that the Corinthians will heed his exhortation and come through on the collection. Paul renounces a direct role in the collection to avoid eliciting criti-

gospel. [19]And not only that, but he has also been appointed our traveling companion by the churches in this gracious work administered by us for the glory of the Lord [himself] and for the expression of our eagerness. [20]This we desire to avoid, that anyone blame us about this lavish gift administered by us, [21]for we are concerned for what is honorable not only in the sight of the Lord but also in the sight of others. [22]And with them we have sent our brother whom we often tested in many ways and found earnest, but who is now much more earnest because of his great confidence in you. [23]As for Titus, he is my partner and co-worker for you; as for our brothers, they are apostles of the churches, the glory of Christ. [24]So give proof before the churches of your love and of our boasting about you to them.

9 God's Indescribable Gift. [1]Now about the service to the holy ones, it is superfluous for me to write to you, [2]for I know your eagerness, about which I boast of you to the Macedonians, that Achaia has been ready since last year; and your zeal has stirred up most of them. [3]Nonetheless, I sent the brothers so that our boast about you might not prove empty in this case, so that you might be ready, as I said, [4]for fear that if any Macedonians come with me and find you not ready we might be put to shame (to say nothing of you) in this conviction. [5]So I thought it necessary to encourage the brothers to go on ahead to you and arrange in advance for your promised gift, so that in this way it might be ready as a bountiful gift and not as an exaction.

[6]Consider this: whoever sows sparingly will also reap sparingly, and whoever sows bountifully will also reap bountifully. [7]Each must do as already determined, without sadness or

---

cism that could undermine the collection (vv. 20-21). Instead, a delegation of three will be sent to Corinth to oversee the project. Paul delegates Titus, who has already had success among the community and is apparently anxious to go back and undertake this task. The identity of the second and third delegates is a matter of speculation. The second is simply referred to as "the brother," someone well known to all the churches and famed for his preaching (v. 18). He has been appointed "by the churches" (v. 19), though Paul does not say which churches. The third delegate, referred to as "our brother," that is, a member of Paul's entourage, is recommended for his earnestness (v. 22).

Paul returns in verse 23 to underscore Titus's status as his co-worker and to qualify the other two delegates as representatives of the churches. If the Corinthians respond enthusiastically with regard to the collection, it will stand as a testimony to their love and be known to all the churches. Moreover, their cooperation will further vindicate Paul's boast, which can only serve to advance and strengthen the reconciliation between Paul and them (v. 24).

compulsion, for God loves a cheerful giver. ⁸Moreover, God is able to make every grace abundant for you, so that in all things, always having all you need, you may have an abundance for every good work. ⁹As it is written:

> "He scatters abroad, he gives to
> the poor;
> his righteousness endures
> forever."

¹⁰The one who supplies seed to the sower and bread for food will supply and multiply your seed and increase the harvest of your righteousness.

¹¹You are being enriched in every way for all generosity, which through us produces thanksgiving to God, ¹²for the ▶ administration of this public service is not only supplying the needs of the holy ones but is also overflowing in many

---

At 9:1 Paul now protests that it is superfluous to write to the Corinthians about the collection for the saints. It is not necessary to assume that this statement signals the start of a new, once originally independent letter. On further consideration, it becomes apparent that the mention of the collection allows Paul to reintroduce the topic of the Macedonians, but in such a way as to instigate the Corinthians to get onboard with the collection and cooperate with the delegates. Paul says that he has boasted to the Macedonians of the Corinthians' year-old eagerness to participate in the collection. He also reports that the Corinthians' example stirred the Macedonians' zeal for the collection and prompted them to contribute (v. 3). In fact, both Paul and the Corinthians know that they had done next to nothing about the collection since the previous year. Thus Paul gives the Corinthians fair warning that with the arrival of the advance delegation in Corinth, they had better expedite the project and be ready for Paul's arrival in the event that any Macedonians accompany Paul (vv. 3-4). Failure on the Corinthians' part would bring shame not only on themselves for being less generous than the poorer Macedonians, but on Paul too (v. 4). Yet Paul is hopeful that motives other than the desire to avoid shame will induce the proud Corinthians to attend earnestly to the collection. This is why he has sent an advance delegation. Their purpose is to encourage and help the Corinthians arrange for their "promised gift" so that it will be ready as a "bountiful gift" and not a last-minute act of begrudging giving (exaction) in order to save face (9:5).

9:6-15 The rewards of giving

Paul now offers a theological foundation, supported by scriptural citations, for his collection project. Picking up on the term "bountiful," he begins with a commonsense statement about sowing and harvesting (v. 6). Applied metaphorically to the topic of giving, what Paul suggests is that bountiful giving will produce bountiful rewards. But if generosity has its

acts of thanksgiving to God. ¹³Through the evidence of this service, you are glorifying God for your obedient confession of the gospel of Christ and the generosity of your contribution to them and to all others, ¹⁴while in prayer on your behalf they long for you, because of the surpassing grace of God upon you. ¹⁵Thanks be to God for his indescribable gift!

Iv. Paul's Defense of His Ministry

10 **Accusation of Weakness.** ¹Now I myself, Paul, urge you through the gentleness and clemency of Christ, I who am humble when face to face with you, but brave toward you when absent, ²I beg you that, when present, I may not have to be brave with that confidence

own rewards, the Corinthians need to realize that generous giving is made possible by God, who first provides the abundance, so that with their own needs met, the Corinthians can give from their abundance (v. 8). This statement reinforces the theological idea already present at 8:1-7, namely, that God is the one who graces/gifts and whose grace enables our gracious giving. That God is the source of all good works is reinforced at verse 9 with a citation from Psalm 111:9 and further reinforced in verse 10a, where the influence of Isaiah 55:10-11 is discernible. Here God is described as not only supplying the seed (grace), that is, creating the possibility of giving, but sustaining this good work of giving by continually multiplying the seed and increasing the "harvest of your righteousness" (v. 10; see Hos 12:10).

At verse 11, Paul reminds the Corinthians that they have already been richly endowed precisely for the sake of being generous "through us," that is, Paul and his collection project. Once the collection is distributed and the poor are assisted, they will give thanks to God for the generosity of the Corinthians, which God has enabled (v. 12), and ultimately God will be glorified (v. 13). Thus the Corinthians are again exhorted to contribute to the collection, not only for their own advantage but because in doing so they demonstrate their obedience to the gospel (v. 13). This authentic expression of Christianity, manifested in generous giving, will bring forth thanks to God for "his indescribable gift" (v. 15).

PAUL'S COUNTERATTACK ON THE INTRUDERS

2 Corinthians 10:1–13:10

Apart from some indirect gibes and insinuations apparently aimed at the rival apostles (see, e.g., 2:17; 3:1; 4:2; 7:2), Paul's primary focus up to this point in the letter has been his conflicted relationship with the community. His goal has been to overcome their differences and restore trust; in con-

with which I intend to act boldly against some who consider us as acting according to the flesh. ³For, although

we are in the flesh, we do not battle according to the flesh, ⁴for the weapons of our battle are not of flesh but are enor-

---

sequence, Paul was able to renew his appeal to the Corinthians concerning the collection. Now he turns to confront the intruders, who were attempting to upstage him and capitalize on the strained relationship to promote themselves.

This final unit serves as a kind of rhetorical knockout punch, packed with invective and sarcasm. Paul refutes accusations leveled against him (10:1-18) and positively contrasts himself with his rivals, who are exposed as charlatans (11:1–12:10). Paul then recaps his major points and brings up the subject of his imminent third visit to Corinth (12:11-21). With the mention of the visit, Paul transitions to the final chapter, where he issues a series of warnings to the community (13:1-10), which are followed by the epistolary conclusion (13:11-13). Throughout this unit Paul takes on his rivals, but his remarks are addressed to the Corinthians. Ultimately, his concern is to safeguard this community and bring about their obedience to the gospel so that when he returns to Corinth, he and they may again enjoy full partnership.

Paul refutes his opponents' accusations (10:1-18)

Two subunits are distinguishable in this opening segment of Paul's argument. The first, verses 1-11, begins and ends with the intruders' criticism of Paul in regard to rhetorical competence. In the second subunit, verses 12-18, Paul is concerned about territorial jurisdiction, around which he develops the theme of boasting in preparation for chapters 11–12.

10:1-11 Spiritual weapons

Paul begins with an exhortation, pointing to the gentleness and clemency of Christ (v. 1a), but quickly alludes to a criticism brought forth by his opponents (v. 1b). Paul denies that he lacks boldness. If he is meek and humble, it is in imitation of Christ. But he is quite prepared to deal boldly with his opponents, who claim that he walks "according to the flesh" (v. 2). In Paul, this phrase usually means to live a sinful life. However, beginning in verse 3, the context requires that the phrase be taken to mean according to human arguments/persuasive strategies. Paul renounces such cunning (see 4:2) and battles with spiritual weapons (literally "weapons powerful to God"), which will be so effective against the slick but vacuous arguments of

mously powerful, capable of destroying fortresses. We destroy arguments [5]and every pretension raising itself against the knowledge of God, and take every thought captive in obedience to Christ, [6]and we are ready to punish every disobedience, once your obedience is complete.

[7]Look at what confronts you. Whoever is confident of belonging to Christ should consider that as he belongs to Christ, so do we. [8]And even if I should boast a little too much of our authority, which the Lord gave for building you up and not for tearing you down, I shall not be put to shame. [9]May I not seem as one frightening you through letters. [10]For someone will say, "His letters are severe and forceful, but his bodily presence is weak, and his speech contemptible." [11]Such a person must understand that what we are in word through letters when absent, that we also are in action when present.

[12]Not that we dare to class or compare ourselves with some of those who

his opponents that Paul will take every thought captive in obedience to Christ (vv. 4-5). In this battle Paul expects to overpower his smooth-talking opponents and win back the Corinthians to complete obedience to Christ, which also means full fellowship with Paul. When this occurs, Paul will punish his opponents, who subvert the gospel (v. 6).

As Paul continues, he commands the Corinthians to face the facts (v. 7a). It is doubtful that someone has accused him of not being Christian; rather, Paul's opponents probably alleged that he was not a true apostle and hence without authority. This seems to be supported by verse 8, where Paul boasts of the authority given him by the Lord. If the opponents were connected to the Jerusalem church, they may have claimed that they were possibly commissioned by Jesus himself (see 5:16) during his earthly ministry or by his immediate disciples. Since Paul cannot claim to have received his apostolic commission in this way, his opponents may have used this fact to discredit his apostolic legitimacy. Yet Paul insists that his claim to be "of Christ" is valid, and his exercise of apostolic authority is genuine, since it is ordered to building up the community (v. 8).

In verses 9-11, Paul returns to allegations concerning his weak personal presence and lack of rhetorical competence and assures the Corinthians that when he arrives, the allegations will be shown to be baseless.

10:12-18 Paul boasts in his own labors

After his ironic jab at his self-commending opponents (v. 12a), who use only one another as a basis of comparison and risk deluding themselves (v. 12b), Paul criticizes his opponents for overstepping boundaries by coming to Corinth to minister. This is not just a matter of guarding his own turf for

recommend themselves. But when they measure themselves by one another and compare themselves with one another, they are without understanding. ¹³But we will not boast beyond measure but will keep to the limits God has apportioned us, namely, to reach even to you. ¹⁴For we are not overreaching ourselves, as though we did not reach you; we indeed first came to you with the gospel of Christ. ¹⁵We are not boasting beyond measure, in other people's labors; yet our hope is that, as your faith increases, our influence among you may be greatly enlarged, within our proper limits, ¹⁶so that we may preach the gospel even beyond you, not boasting of work already done in another's sphere. ¹⁷"Whoever boasts, should boast in the Lord." ¹⁸For it is not the one who recommends himself who is approved, but the one whom the Lord recommends.

11 **Preaching without Charge.** ¹If only you would put up with a little foolishness from me! Please put up with me. ²For I am jealous of you with ▶

selfish reasons. Corinth, a Gentile city, was part of Paul's ministerial jurisdiction to the Gentiles, apportioned to him and his co-workers by God (v. 13) and confirmed by the apostles at the Jerusalem council (see Gal 2:6-10).

Apparently, in Paul's mind the two broad ministerial jurisdictions established at this council along ethnic lines of demarcation—one for the circumcised/Jews, the other for the Gentiles—also implied geographical lines of demarcation. Unlike his opponents, who did not honor these boundaries, Paul did not overreach his territorial limits (v. 14) or build on anyone else's labors (v. 15). Thus Paul, who is approved by the Lord and whose work has been done within the limits established by God, is the one with the legitimate right to boast in what has been accomplished at Corinth (v. 17-18).

The "fool's speech" (11:1–12:10)

In view of the recurrence of the words "fool," "foolishness," and "foolish," this segment of Paul's argument is usually referred to as the "fool's speech." Paul first explains why it is necessary that he engage in a little foolishness (11:1-21a) and then indulges in his own foolish boasting (11:16–12:10). Throughout this speech Paul deftly uses the rhetorical skill he was said to lack to deride his opponents and their claims.

11:1-21a A "little foolishness"

Though Paul considers boasting foolishness, he finds it necessary to engage in a "little foolishness" (v. 1) of his own, since the Corinthians not only tolerate the boasting of his opponents but also are swayed by them to accept a different gospel to their own peril (v. 4). Like the father of a bride, responsible for safeguarding the virginity of his daughter until she wed

the jealousy of God, since I betrothed you to one husband to present you as a chaste virgin to Christ. ³But I am afraid that, as the serpent deceived Eve by his cunning, your thoughts may be corrupted from a sincere [and pure] commitment to Christ. ⁴For if someone comes and preaches another Jesus than the one we preached, or if you receive a different spirit from the one you received or a different gospel from the one you accepted, you put up with it well enough. ⁵For I think that I am not in any way inferior to these "superapostles." ⁶Even if I am untrained in speaking, I am not so in knowledge; in every way we have made this plain to you in all things.

⁷Did I make a mistake when I humbled myself so that you might be exalted, because I preached the gospel of God to you without charge? ⁸I plundered other churches by accepting from them in order to minister to you. ⁹And when I was with you and in need, I did not burden anyone, for the brothers who came from Macedonia supplied my needs. So I refrained and will refrain from burdening you in any way. ¹⁰By the truth of Christ in me, this boast of mine shall not be silenced in the regions of Achaia. ¹¹And why? Because I do not love you? God knows I do!

¹²And what I do I will continue to do, in order to end this pretext of those who

---

her betrothed, Paul's apostolic task is to preserve the community incorrupt for Christ alone. However, he fears that like Eve, seduced and deceived by Satan disguised as a serpent, the community was allowing itself to be seduced and corrupted by these superapostles. In comparison with these, Paul is in no way inferior (v. 5). Though he concedes that he lacks training in the art of oratory, he denies lacking knowledge, which he has abundantly demonstrated (v. 6).

In bringing up his practice of preaching the gospel free of charge (v. 7), Paul seems to have abruptly changed topics. However, this issue is closely linked to the charge of inferiority, since in Paul's day it was assumed that preachers without financial backing were second-rate. Paul now appears to be second-guessing himself, questioning whether his choice was a mistake, since it could be cited as further proof of his inferiority. If he were a true apostle, he should have taken the support due to him. He had already explained why he renounced his apostolic right to financial support (1 Cor 9) and does not repeat those reasons here. Here he simply asserts that he has not and will not burden the Corinthians (v. 9).

That the Corinthians continue to find grounds in this for despising Paul as inferior is not his problem. He will not allow his preaching of the gospel to be compromised by the patronage system and intends to boast of his independence from such social conventions. And he will continue to operate this way! This is not because he disdains the Corinthians,

seek a pretext for being regarded as we are in the mission of which they boast. [13]For such people are false apostles, deceitful workers, who masquerade as apostles of Christ. [14]And no wonder, for even Satan masquerades as an angel of light. [15]So it is not strange that his ministers also masquerade as ministers of righteousness. Their end will correspond to their deeds.

Paul's Boast: His Labors. [16]I repeat, no one should consider me foolish; but if you do, accept me as a fool, so that I too may boast a little. [17]What I am saying I am not saying according to the Lord but as in foolishness, in this boastful state. [18]Since many boast according to the flesh, I too will boast. [19]For you gladly put up with fools, since you are wise yourselves. [20]For you put up with it if someone enslaves you, or devours you, or gets the better of you, or puts on airs, or slaps you in the face. [21]To my shame I say that we were too weak!

But what anyone dares to boast of (I am speaking in foolishness) I also dare.

---

whom he assures of his love (v. 11). Rather, his goal is to stop the superapostles from using the Corinthians' financial support to feign friendship and manipulate allegiance when their real intention is to supplant Paul and boast of the successful mission at Corinth as if it were the result of their work and not his (v. 12). Paul's verbal assault on these predators is vehement. He rejects them as false apostles and deceivers. Masquerading as apostles of Christ, they are actually ministers of Satan. According to Jewish tradition, Satan disguised himself as an angel of light (see *Apocalypse of Moses* 17:1-2). Thus, like Satan, so his followers. Paul concludes this tirade with a short eschatological statement obviously intended as a threat. In the end, they will be unmasked, and their judgment will correspond to their deeds.

After ten verses of defense and attack, Paul reminds his readers that he is going to begin his "fool's speech," even though it goes against his own better judgment (v. 16). The circumstances require that he take on the role of a boaster. By doing this, he risks being considered foolish, but he fears far greater risks to the community if he does not. The Corinthians should be able to deal with him in this assumed role, since they gladly put up with *real* fools (v. 19)! This stinging sarcasm continues as Paul describes the excessive tolerance of the "wise" Corinthians, who put up with the worst abuses at the hands of their ministers (v. 20)! Paul's mocking depiction of the Corinthians as gullible pawns is intended to force them to realize how foolish is their attachment to his opponents, who actually victimize the community. Paul concludes with an admission of weakness, but this is probably intended ironically, since he is about to boast quite boldly.

²²Are they Hebrews? So am I. Are they Israelites? So am I. Are they descendants of Abraham? So am I. ²³Are they ministers of Christ? (I am talking like an insane person.) I am still more, with far greater labors, far more imprisonments, far worse beatings, and numerous brushes with death. ²⁴Five times at

---

11:21b–12:10 Paul's foolish boasting

The fool's speech proper begins here. The agenda for this bragging contest is set by the opponents. Whatever they dare boast of, Paul will too (v. 21b). The contest begins with a focus on titles. On the first point, Paul can equally claim the three titles Hebrew, Israelite, descendant of Abraham, which are claimed with boastful pride by his opponents (v. 22). Ethnically, culturally, and religiously, there is simply no disparity between himself and the rivals.

When it comes to the next title, "ministers of Christ," Paul ironically stakes his claim to this title, not on powerful deeds or notable accomplishments, as his rivals did, but on suffering—and Paul's were unparalleled (v. 23b)! He lists them in spades, bragging about all the dangers, hardships, beatings, deprivation, and humiliation he has endured throughout his ministry (vv. 24-28). All this suffering, which had been cited by his opponents to discredit his apostolic authority and ministry, Paul now shamelessly showcases as that which legitimates his claim to the title "minister of Christ." Paul is clearly the supersufferer! Since suffering and affliction, paradoxically, constitute the credentials of a true apostle and authentic minister (see 4:7– 5:10), the Corinthians should recognize Paul's apostolic legitimacy.

In this clever and ironic twist, Paul has pulled the rug out from under his opponents, who consider demonstrations of power authenticators of apostolic ministry. Paul knows very well that his opponents would never admit of, let alone boast of, weakness, even if they had suffered! Thus the irony of his question, "Who is weak, and I am not weak?" (v. 29)!

Since Paul must boast, he boasts of another episode of weakness and indignity—his escape from Damascus (vv. 30-33; see also Acts 9:23-25). His purpose in adding this particular example to the catalogue of hardships already recited is illumined by the contemporary Roman military practice of awarding the "wall crown" to the first soldier to scale the enemy's wall. By contrast, Paul is but a weakling, an anti-hero being shuttled down the wall in a basket! Paul's intentional spoof on the practice of recognizing and rewarding displays of power is a perfect lead-in to the last item of comparison in the fool's speech (12:1-10).

the hands of the Jews I received forty lashes minus one. ²⁵Three times I was beaten with rods, once I was stoned, three times I was shipwrecked, I passed a night and a day on the deep; ²⁶on frequent journeys, in dangers from rivers, dangers from robbers, dangers from my own race, dangers from Gentiles, dangers in the city, dangers in the wilderness, dangers at sea, dangers among false brothers; ²⁷in toil and hardship, through many sleepless nights, through hunger and thirst, through frequent fastings, through cold and exposure. ²⁸And apart from these things, there is the daily pressure upon me of my anxiety for all the churches. ²⁹Who is weak, and I am not weak? Who is led to sin, and I am not indignant?

Paul's Boast: His Weakness. ³⁰If I must boast, I will boast of the things that show my weakness. ³¹The God and Father of the Lord Jesus knows, he who is blessed forever, that I do not lie. ³²At Damascus, the governor under King Aretas guarded the city of Damascus, in order to seize me, ³³but I was lowered in a basket through a window in the wall and escaped his hands.

12 ¹I must boast; not that it is profitable, but I will go on to visions and revelations of the Lord. ²I know someone in Christ who, fourteen years ago (whether in the body or out of the body I do not know, God knows), was caught up to the third heaven. ³And I know that this person (whether in the body or out of the body I do not know,

---

Apparently the superapostles had impressed the Corinthians with displays of spiritual power and descriptions of ecstatic experiences. Paul knows that comparing such experiences serves no purpose (v. 1), since weakness, rather than displays of power, authenticates ministry. However, having been forced into this boasting contest, Paul has no choice but to recount a revelatory experience of his own. His reluctance is evident in the fact that he speaks in the third person. This is a rhetorical device that allows him to distance himself from this visionary episode, which, though extraordinary, has little to do with the authenticity of his daily ministry. Only God knows how "this person" was transported to Paradise, the highest of heavens, where he was granted special revelations meant to be kept secret (vv. 3-4). About "this person" Paul has reason to boast (v. 5), since he has been granted access to a place few have been permitted to enter and has been privy to ineffable revelations.

But at this point Paul again subverts the boasting contest by introducing his own terms: "about myself I will not boast, except about my weaknesses" (v. 5b). Were he to boast about his experience to impress the Corinthians, he would be telling the truth, since he has had an "abundance of the revelations" (vv. 6-7a). But he will not boast, because he has been given a "thorn in the flesh." Though the exact nature of this affliction is not certain, its purpose is. Paul twice emphasizes that this "thorn" was given

God knows) [4]was caught up into Paradise and heard ineffable things, which no one may utter. [5]About this person I will boast, but about myself I will not boast, except about my weaknesses. [6]Although if I should wish to boast, I would not be foolish, for I would be telling the truth. But I refrain, so that no one may think more of me than what he sees in me or hears from me [7]because of the abundance of the revelations. Therefore, that I might not become too elated, a thorn in the flesh was given to me, an angel of Satan, to beat me, to keep me from being too elated. [8]Three times I begged the Lord about this, that it might leave me, [9]but he said to me, "My grace is sufficient for you, for power is made perfect in weakness." I will rather boast most gladly of my weaknesses, in order that the power of Christ may dwell with me. [10]Therefore, I am content with weaknesses, insults, hardships, persecutions, and constraints, for the sake of Christ; for when I am weak, then I am strong.

to him precisely to prevent his being "too elated" (v. 7). Paul's thrice-repeated plea that he be relieved of this suffering is reminiscent of Jesus' supplication in the garden (see Matt 26:39-44). The Lord's answer (v. 9), presented as authoritative divine revelation, reminds Paul that the only thing that counts is God's grace—not mystical experiences or human displays of power, but God's grace.

Moreover, God's "power" (v. 9; here a synonym for grace) is brought to perfection in weakness. Thus Paul need not seek to overcome weakness and avoid suffering. When he is weakest, as measured by human standards, he is strongest, not by the dint of his own resources but by the grace/power of God paradoxically manifested in weakness. Rather than despising Paul, the Corinthians ought to recognize that his weakness is powerful testimony that God is at work in their apostle's life and ministry. In light of this revelation, Paul's conclusion makes perfect sense: he will boast of his weakness and be content with his hardships (vv. 10-11).

In the end, even though Paul's revelatory experience ironically turned out to be another affirmation of his weakness, he has won this boasting contest. He has won not on his opponents' terms nor even on his own, but ultimately on God's terms. God manifested his power and wisdom in the weakness and folly of the cross (see 1 Cor 1:18-31), and God continues to do so in the weakness and suffering of his ministers, whose lives are conformed to the life of Jesus (see 4:10-11).

12:11-21 Epilogue and transition

The fool's speech is over, and as if embarrassed by his own peacock performance, Paul reminds the Corinthians that their failure to support him forced him into foolish self-commendation (v. 11). Having excused

Selfless Concern for the Church. [11]I have been foolish. You compelled me, for I ought to have been commended by you. For I am in no way inferior to these "superapostles," even though I am nothing. [12]The signs of an apostle were performed among you with all endurance, signs and wonders, and mighty deeds. [13]In what way were you less privileged than the rest of the churches, except that on my part I did not burden you? Forgive me this wrong!

[14]Now I am ready to come to you this third time. And I will not be a burden, for I want not what is yours, but you. Children ought not to save for their parents, but parents for their children. [15]I will most gladly spend and be utterly spent for your sakes. If I love you more, am I to be loved less? [16]But granted that I myself did not burden you, yet I was crafty and got the better of you by deceit. [17]Did I take advantage of you through any of those I sent to you? [18]I urged Titus to go and sent the brother with him. Did Titus take advantage of you? Did we not walk in the same spirit? And in the same steps?

---

himself, Paul now recaps major points made in the two preceding sections. He is not inferior. Opponents may call him a "nothing," but no number of insults can change the fact that he is a true apostle (v. 11c). Though Paul refrains from saying that he accomplished signs among the Corinthians, he insists that they "were performed among you" (v. 12). The use of the passive may be intended to underscore the power of God at work through the apostle's weakness. Paul then restates his motive for refusing their support (v. 13). His request that they forgive him for this "wrong" is pure sarcasm.

Paul is ready to go back to the community and announces an imminent visit (v. 14a). His founding visit to Corinth was followed by a second, "painful" visit (chs.1–2). This will be his third (v. 14). His refusal to accept their financial support remains a delicate issue. Paul tries to dispel the rancor about his praxis by showing that his motives, unlike those of his opponents, who are indirectly impugned here, are selfless. First he stresses that his interest is in them and not their possessions (14b). Then he points to the customary financial setup between children and parents. In view of this, it is clear that Paul alone behaves as a true parent to the Corinthians, while his opponents subvert this natural order of things by taking. While they live off Paul's spiritual children, he is impelled by his profound love for the Corinthians "to spend" himself and be "spent" for them (vv. 14c-15).

The comparison between Paul and his opponents is implicit in his emotionally charged question, "If I love you more, am I to be loved less? " (v. 15c). If the Corinthians are honest, they will have to admit that they have been shortchanging Paul when it comes to love and support. They will also

Final Warnings and Appeals.
[19]Have you been thinking all along that we are defending ourselves before you? In the sight of God we are speaking in Christ, and all for building you up, beloved. [20]For I fear that when I come I may find you not such as I wish, and that you may find me not as you wish; that there may be rivalry, jealousy, fury, selfishness, slander, gossip, conceit, and disorder. [21]I fear that when I come again my God may humiliate me before you, and I may have to mourn over many of those who sinned earlier and have not repented of the impurity, immorality, and licentiousness they practiced.

13 [1]This third time I am coming to you. "On the testimony of two or three witnesses a fact shall be estab-

---

have to grant that Paul has truly never burdened them (v. 16a). However, Paul knows that his opponents have planted the suspicion that he is deceitfully living off the Corinthians by covertly siphoning money from what they had put aside for the collection (v. 16b). Paul denies doing this. In fact, he has opted out of direct involvement in the collection and is sending Titus (see 8:16-24). On a previous mission to Corinth, Titus had been positively impressed by the Corinthians, who apparently felt comfortable and confident enough with him to admit their error (see 7:5-15). If the community has confidence in Titus, who shares with Paul the "same" values and approach to ministry, to suspect Paul of dishonesty is not only unfounded but also illogical.

Paul knows that what he has said sounds like a defense, and in many ways it has been, but he hastens to add that his testimony before God in Christ (see 2:17) is part of his apostolic service to upbuild the community (see 10:8). Paul's apprehension about this trip derives from concerns about what he may discover upon his return to Corinth. His fear is that the unity and holiness of the community are still being compromised by the same litigious and immoral behavior (vv. 21-22) that he had already addressed in 1 Corinthians. If so, Paul also fears that he may be in for another humiliating experience, comparable to what occurred on his second visit. His announcement of an imminent visit, his expressed fear that the Corinthians had still not conformed their lives to the gospel, and his mention of unrepentant sinners provide the transition to the concluding chapter.

13:1-10 Final warnings

The juridical significance of the qualifier "third" (v. 1a) is made clear in v. 1b, where Paul cites a legal prescription which states that the testimony of at least two or three witnesses is required to convict an alleged wrongdoer (see Deut 19:15). Paul had witnessed wrongdoing and served warning on

lished." [2]I warned those who sinned earlier and all the others, and I warn them now while absent, as I did when present on my second visit, that if I come again I will not be lenient, [3]since you are looking for proof of Christ speaking in me. He is not weak toward you but powerful in you. [4]For indeed he was crucified ▶ out of weakness, but he lives by the power of God. So also we are weak in

his second visit, which he now repeats in absentia (v. 2a). Should he again find anyone persisting in wrongdoing on this third visit, Paul's case against the wrongdoers would be conclusively established (v. 2b). Paul will not be lenient in dealing with unrepentant sinners and offers this as proof to the community that Christ is speaking through him (vv. 2c-3a). As Paul's weakness testified to his conformity to Christ, so also does his power. Paul will come in the power of Christ and deal boldly with the Corinthians (v. 4).

In the next series of admonitions (vv. 5-9), Paul, who has been under intense scrutiny with regard to his apostolic authenticity, turns the tables and admonishes the Corinthians to scrutinize themselves about their own authenticity. Examine and test yourselves, Paul cautions. Are you living in the faith, that is, do your lives conform to the gospel? Would your lives show that Christ is in you?

Though Paul expresses himself in a somewhat convoluted way in verses 6-9, the import of these statements is this: what the Corinthians think of Paul is less important than whether they advance in their life in Christ and commitment to the gospel. If this occurs, it does not matter to Paul whether or not he is judged an authentic apostle by their criteria. He has acted according to the truth and rejoices when the Corinthians are strong even if he is weak. Paul can and does pray for the community. However, in the end it is up to the Corinthians to renew their commitment to Christ and to live as true Christians. Paul's hope is that this severe written warning will be effective. Otherwise, despite claims to the contrary (see 10:10), Paul will be severe when he is again present among them and will exercise his apostolic authority to build up this community, which risks destroying itself.

EPISTOLARY CONCLUSION

2 Corinthians 13:11-13

After bidding the Corinthians to rejoice, Paul exhorts them to mend their ways, encourage one another, agree with one another, and live in peace (v. 11). These exhortations recall the situation of 1 Corinthians, where Paul had to deal with immoral lives in need of reform (1 Cor 5–6);

him, but toward you we shall live with him by the power of God.

⁵Examine yourselves to see whether you are living in faith. Test yourselves. Do you not realize that Jesus Christ is in you?—unless, of course, you fail the test. ⁶I hope you will discover that we have not failed. ⁷But we pray to God that you may not do evil, not that we may appear to have passed the test but that you may do what is right, even though we may seem to have failed. ⁸For we cannot do anything against the truth, but only for the truth. ⁹For we rejoice when we are weak but you are strong. What we pray for is your improvement.

¹⁰I am writing this while I am away, so that when I come I may not have to be severe in virtue of the authority that the Lord has given me to build up and not to tear down.

v. Conclusion

¹¹Finally, brothers, rejoice. Mend your ways, encourage one another, agree with one another, live in peace, and the God of love and peace will be with you. ¹²Greet one another with a holy kiss. All the holy ones greet you. ¹³The grace of the Lord Jesus Christ and the love of God and the fellowship of the holy Spirit be with all of you.

---

disedifying rather than mutually upbuilding behavior (1 Cor 8–10); disagreement (1 Cor 1–4); and discord (1 Cor 12–14). The reader who gets the impression that the situation at Corinth has not significantly improved is probably right. Paul has tirelessly preached the gospel and labored to create a community of believers at Corinth. In the end, though, it is the responsibility of each believer to make Christian community a reality at Corinth. Whether Paul is absent or present, the Corinthians, who are Paul's partners in the work of the gospel, are responsible for the continual renewal of their lives and the work of reconciliation (see 5:17-20). Once they are a community of love and peace, then the God of love and peace will dwell among them.

After hearing this letter read to them, the Corinthians were to exchange a "holy kiss," a symbol of each member's willingness to heed Paul's exhortation and to work toward unity and reconciliation. Paul typically closes his letters with a blessing, but this is the only time he invokes the blessings of the Lord Jesus Christ, God, and the holy Spirit (v. 14). While the prayer is Trinitarian in structure, it does not necessarily express all that is understood about the nature of God as enunciated in the doctrine of the Trinity. In the context of this letter, what the prayer does express is Paul's sincere desire that through the outpouring of Christ's grace, through which the community has come to know the love of God, they may live in the fellowship of the holy Spirit, who indwells each of them and is the source and sustainer of their unity in Christ.

REVIEW AIDS AND DISCUSSION TOPICS

Introduction *(pages 5–16)*

1. What were the characteristics of the church at Corinth? Does this description have any relevance for Christian communities today?

2. What is the significance of the location of Corinth for understanding the times, character, circumstances, and message of the First Letter to the Corinthians? What did the religious picture of Corinth look like? Does Corinth resemble the great cities of today? If so, how?

3. First Corinthians addresses many concrete problems proper to the first century. Do you think its value for us is limited? If so, why? If not, how is it applicable today?

First Letter to the Corinthians

1:1-9 Introduction *(pages 17–21)*

1. How does Paul understand himself in relation to Christ?

2. What are the four qualifications by which Paul distinguishes the Corinthian community? Do you think they apply to your community/parish?

3. Despite the problems besetting the church at Corinth, Paul expresses thanks for the Corinthians and the grace they have received. Why? What does Paul's thankfulness and confidence say to you regarding the problems besetting the church today?

1:10–4:21 Argument for Unity in the Community *(pages 21–36)*

1. What is the paradox of the cross? How has that paradox manifested itself in the Corinthian church? Have you experienced the paradox of the cross in your own life? How?

2. What does Paul mean by spiritual maturity? Paul says the Corinthians are not spiritually mature. Why?

3. Paul says the Corinthians continue to admire and to seek the wisdom of the world. What are the effects of this in the community? Do you

think Christians today are still seeking "worldly" wisdom? If so, what are some of the effects?

4. What, according to Paul, is the most important quality in the minister? What does he mean by it? Do you agree? If so, why? If not, what quality do you think is most important and why?

5:1–6:20 Arguments Concerning Immorality within the Community and Relationships with Those outside the Community *(pages 36–46)*

1. Is Paul too harsh in his reaction to the reports about the incestuous man (5:1-13)? Why? Is he harsh because the sin is sexual? How does this case relate to Paul's reflections on the "temple of God" (3:16-17)?

2. Why does Paul take the Corinthians to task for having recourse to pagan courts (6:1-11)? Is there any way Paul's lesson concerning the courts could be applicable today?

3. What is Paul's teaching regarding the Corinthians' freedom as Christians? Does his teaching regarding the individual Christian as the temple of the Holy Spirit have application beyond the sexual sphere? If so, how? If no, why not?

7:1-40 Concerning Marriage and Sexual Relations *(pages 46–52)*

1. What is the major influence on Paul's opinions regarding these matters? Do you think it important to keep this in mind when discussing Paul's teachings in verses 1-16 and 25-40? Why?

2. Is Paul for or against marriage? Does he have a healthy perspective on human sexuality? Why?

3. Is Paul for or against slavery? Why does Paul advocate no change in the status quo? Can this be applicable today? How? Why?

8:1–11:1 Argument Concerning Food Offered to Idols *(pages 52–62)*

1. How does the issue of idol-meats affect the Christian community at Corinth? Is an individual's conscience absolute and autonomous? Is this section (8:1-13) on food offered to idols obsolete today, or are there ways in which our church could apply its meaning?

2. Does Paul's self-description of "being all things to all" (9:19-23) strike you as hypocritical? Why? How is what he describes different from crowd-pleasing or human respect? Is this compatible with freedom and self-determination?

3. Do the "strong" have any parallels today? How can they be reconciled with the "weak"? Does Paul provide any critique we might be able to apply to Eucharistic celebrations today?

11:2–14:40 Arguments Concerning Aspects of Community Worship *(pages 62–83)*

1. Does Paul prohibit anyone from any liturgical roles? Why does he bother to deal with the issue of liturgical dress? What is the relationship of 11:2-16 to its context (i.e., 10:23–11:1 and 11:17-34)? Does the church follow Paul's teaching in its attitude toward the ministry of women today?

2. What abuses of the Eucharist does Paul address (11:17-22)? What are the possible meanings of the phrase "body of Christ" (or "of the Lord") in this context (e.g., 1 Cor 11:24, 27, 29; see 12:12-31)? Are they mutually exclusive? Do you think Paul's teaching on the Eucharist has application to our Eucharistic celebrations today? If so, how? If not, why not?

3. What is the problem about spiritual gifts in Corinth? Are there some gifts or functions in the church today which seem to be more desirable than others? What does Paul say about the gift of tongues relative to other gifts? What do you think the place of the priesthood is within any discussion of gifts? What is the place of chapter 13 in this discussion?

4. How does Paul approach the question of regulating the Spirit? Is there any way to apply this today? Should women speak about religion exclusively at home and then by acknowledging their husbands as the sole authority (14:34-35, but see 11:5)? How can we interpret Paul on this question for today? Should the church be governed by the cultural norms of Paul's time and of the community to which he was writing?

15:1-58 Argument for the Resurrection *(pages 83–91)*

1. In what ways could the problems experienced by the Corinthians, discussed by Paul in earlier chapters, have prompted Paul to recall for them his teaching on the resurrection? What is this teaching? What are Paul's sources?

2. Why is the Corinthian position on the resurrection absurd? How is Paul's position the only reasonable alternative? If Paul has seen the

risen Jesus, why does he insist that the resurrection is the basis of faith, which is trusting in that which one has never seen? Do you think the creed Paul repeats in 15:3b-5 is the core of Christian belief? Why?

3. What is Paul's teaching regarding the nature of the resurrection body? Why is belief in Christ's resurrection and the resurrection of believers so important? What are the implications of this belief for the Corinthians' and our lives? Has there ever been a time when your belief in the resurrection has made an important difference in something you have done or not done?

16:1-24 Conclusion *(pages 91–95)*

1. According to Paul, why should the Gentile Christians contribute to a collection for the Jewish Christians in Jerusalem? Does Paul's discussion of the collection have any application for us today?

2. If Paul is trying to reinforce in verses 19-20 the sense that all believers everywhere are joined in one new family of faith, what does that say about how we greet strangers at our Eucharistic and other assemblies, no matter how different they are from us?

Second Letter to the Corinthians

Introduction *(pages 97–101)*

1. Why did Paul write this letter to the Corinthians? What sort of people do you think the "intruders" were? Do you think Paul was justified in reacting so strongly?

2. What are the key theological ideas in Second Corinthians? Do you think they are as valid today as they were when Paul wrote his letter?

1:1-11 Introduction *(pages 103–105)*

1. According to Paul, what is the purpose of his suffering? Is suffering a sign of weakness? Do you know anyone who considers mental/spiritual suffering a kind of weakness? How would you answer such a person?

2. The word translated here as "encouragement" can also be translated as "comfort." Does the substitution of "comfort" in verses 3-7 change your understanding of this passage? If so, how?

1:12–2:16 Paul's True Motives and Character *(pages 105–110)*

1. What is the apparent accusation of the Corinthians against Paul (1:12-23)? Besides Paul's personal hurt, what is the real danger he perceives in this accusation which prompts him to react so strongly? Do you find Paul's defense of his trustworthiness in 1:18-22 convincing?

2. Have you ever belonged to a group (for instance, a club or your family) that has had to "excommunicate" a member because of something that person has done? How did it affect the group? the offender? Do you think it helped the person, the unity of the group? Or did it split the group?

2:17–7:16 Paul Defends His Ministry *(pages 110–125)*

1. How does Paul contrast the old and new covenant (3:3-18)? What are some of the implications of this contrast for Paul's authority compared to Moses'? How do you think this would have struck Jewish Christians? Why do you think Paul so strongly disparaged the Law? How do you see the Law in relation to Christianity?

2. What is the paradoxical nature of authentic Christian ministry according to Paul (4:7–5:10)? Have you ever had the experience of God working in you when you were convinced you were not equal to the task before you?

3. If Christ died for us, what are the implications of that death for us (5:14-17)? If Christ, through his death, has reconciled all creation with God, how can we live out that reconciliation in our lives? What can Paul's defense of himself in 6:3-10 tell us about judging those who declare themselves to be "authentic" ministers of the gospel and qualified to judge those who are "saved" and those who are not, who declare they can judge whether or not we or others are reconciled with God?

4. Give some examples of how the ministry of reconciliation can be carried out in the world by Christians today (see 2 Cor 5:17-20). How does Paul express his confidence that he has been reconciled with the Corinthians (see 5:11–7:16)? Where do you think reconciliation is most needed in the world today?

8:1–9:15 The Collection for Jerusalem *(pages 127–132)*

1. It is obvious that Paul's relationship with the Corinthians is fragile. After having spent so much time reestablishing the relationship and

effecting a reconciliation, why do you think he introduces so delicate a subject as the collection of money? How does Paul practice diplomacy in his discussion of the collection? Do you think his sending representatives, rather than coming himself, is a wise move?

2. Why is so much attention given to the collection? Is Paul mercenary? What are some motivations for generous giving according to Paul?

10:1–13:10 Paul's Counterattack on the Intruders *(pages 132–143)*

1. How does Paul respond to the charge that he is an inferior apostle (e.g., 10:7-18; 11:4-6)? That he is weak? On what are these charges apparently based? What is the role of suffering in substantiating Paul's claim to apostleship (11:18-28)?

2. Why is the issue of Paul's refusing support from the Corinthians so important (11:7-18)? How does Paul compare with the "superapostles" (11:5)? What is the meaning of God's power being made perfect in weakness (12:9)? How do you understand Paul's "thorn in the flesh" (12:7)?

3. Do you think the situation has changed much in Corinth since Paul wrote his first letter to the Corinthians? Do you think the Corinthian community resembles the church today? If so, how? If not, why? What lessons do you think we, as a church, can learn from the Corinthian community and its relationship with Paul?

13:11-13 Epistolary Conclusion *(pages 143–144)*

1. What do verses 11-12 say to you about our part in bringing unity and peace to the church? Paul says the Corinthians should "greet one another with a holy kiss"? What does this say to you about how we should approach the Kiss of Peace during the celebration of the Eucharist? Do you think we take the Kiss of Peace as seriously as we should?

2. Do you think this letter is valuable for us today?